HOW TO HANDLE THE
NEWS MEDIA

Also by Wanda Vassallo:

Speaking with Confidence
A Parable a Day Keeps the Devil at Bay
A Parable a Day Helps Me Trust and Obey

HOW TO HANDLE THE
NEWS MEDIA

Wanda Vassallo and Dean Angel

BETTERWAY BOOKS
Cincinnati, Ohio

Cover design by Rick Britton
Typography by Park Lane Associates

Cartoon on pages 36-37 reprinted with special permission of North
America Syndicate.
Cartoons on pages 38-39, 60-61, 66, and 97 reprinted by permission: Trib-
une Media Services.
Cartoon on page 106 reprinted with permission of Bill DeOre.
Cartoon on page 47 reprinted with permission of Don Wright, *The Palm
Beach Post*.

97 96 95 94 93   5 4 3 2 1

Library of Congress Cataloging-in-Publication Data

Vassallo, Wanda.
        How to handle the news media / Wanda Vassallo and Dean Angel.
            p. cm.
        Includes bibliographical references and index.
        ISBN 1-55870-251-2 (pbk.) : $7.95
            1. Television broadcasting of news. 2. Interviewing in journalism.
        3. Interviewing in television. I. Angel, Dean.
        II. Title.
        PN4888.T4V37 1992
        302.23'45--dc20   92-16999
                                                                                        CIP

*For Leslie Angel
and
Larry Ballard*

Acknowledgments

With appreciation to the librarians at the Dallas Public
Central Library for their excellent research assistance.

Contents

Introduction

Abraham Lincoln said: "Public sentiment is everything. With public sentiment nothing can fail; without it nothing can succeed. Consequently, he who molds public sentiment goes deeper than he who enacts statutes or pronounces decisions."[1]

There is no doubt that the major molder of public sentiment today is the news media. For better or worse, our opinions are forged, our perspectives shaped, our emotions swayed by what editors and reporters decide should be in our daily information diet. Theirs is a powerful position ... and an awesome responsibility.

Perhaps you, like most Americans, cannot start your day without reading your newspaper and cannot end it without seeing the evening news. After all, you must stay informed. But how are you informed? What is the process behind the slick television newscast with the urbane, witty news anchors and the front page of the newspaper that you welcome into your home as an old and trusted friend?

Our threefold purpose in writing this book is:

1. To explain the inner workings of the news-making process,
2. To prepare you to handle a news media interview or similar situation to your best advantage,
3. To assist you in working with the news media to get your message across to the public.

Whether you are the administrator of a hospital, the newly elected publicity chairperson of your garden club, a member of city council, the auction chairperson for your civic organization, a religious group secretary, a citizen running for public office, a chamber of commerce manager, an author, a school principal, the owner of a small business, or just a private citizen, at some time you will probably find yourself in direct contact with a representative of the news media. Whether that contact is by design when you wish to publicize your organization, an upcoming event, or yourself; or as a result of an emergency, controversy, disaster, or unusual happenstance, the information in this book will help you to come out looking your best. So read it, and smile when someone says, "Here comes that reporter again."

Pre-Test

Answer the following questions with true or false. Read the book, then retake the test. Answers, along with brief explanations, are found on page 142.

1. Legally you can ask a reporter to leave a rally you are conducting in a city park.
2. If you do not want to answer a question, it is best to say, "No comment."
3. Legally a reporter can be barred from a public school classroom if the administrator believes his or her presence would be disruptive to the learning process.
4. You should look at the reporter rather than the camera during a television interview.
5. A good way to postpone a negative story is to wait until the reporter's deadline is past before returning his or her phone call.
6. Every news story will usually contain at least one mistake.
7. To ensure that there are no errors, be sure to ask to see the story before the public does.
8. It is all right to give a reporter confidential information if you explain that you are speaking "off the record."
9. The average television news story is less than a minute in length.
10. The front page of a newspaper contains the most widely-read articles.
11. It is better to answer a reporter's question with a simple "yes" or "no" than to try to explain.
12. In a television interview, you should take the microphone to ensure that every word can be heard.

1

What is News?

... news is not a mirror of social conditions, but the report of an aspect which has obtruded itself. The news does not tell you how the seed is germinating in the ground, but it may tell you when the first sprout breaks through the surface. It may even tell you what somebody says is happening to the seed under ground. It may tell you that the sprout did not come up at the time it was expected. The more points, then, at which any happening can be fixed, objectified, measured, named, the more points there are at which news can occur. [1]

WALTER LIPPMANN, American journalist
and political analyst

Princess Grace of Monaco once said, "The freedom of the press works in such a way that there is not much freedom from it."[2]

No doubt anyone in the public eye would agree with Princess Grace's statement. But even those who consider themselves in the "private citizen" category may suddenly find the public spotlight shining their way. When that happens, they will probably be faced with an awe-inspiring (and perhaps awful) experience—that of a news reporter shoving a microphone in their face and asking a lot of demanding questions.

Understanding what news is all about, the approaches and needs of different media, and the news media's role in a free society will help to make that kind of experience a more positive one. That insight also will assist those who want news coverage to advance their organization or their own personal goals to get the best and most frequent media coverage possible.

A DEFINITION

News is something out-of-the-ordinary that will happen, that is happening, or that did happen just a minute ago and will interest people beyond those immediately involved.

As the editor of a West Coast daily said: "News is the unusual. Too often, perhaps, news is crime, sensationalism, the exposure of corruption. The editor is *not* interested in the 50 houses in the neighborhood that *didn't* burn down yesterday. He's interested in the one that did."[3]

He is interested in the one that did because you—the reader, listener, and viewer—are interested.

THE NEWS BUSINESS

Newspaper publishers and owners of radio and television stations are business people. Just as in any other business, their existence depends on making a profit. They are in a constant race with their competitors for wider circulation or more listeners or viewers. That is what attracts advertisers and determines the rates they can charge. While reporting the news can be considered a service to the public, it also boils down to a bottom-line consideration of profit or loss.

All of us have probably said at one time or another, "Why don't they ever put anything good on the news?" Of course, there are feature stories and human interest reports that fall into the good news category. But ask yourself, "Would I watch the ten o'clock news if that was all they reported?" Probably not.

Ask Ted Turner how interested people really are in good news. His cable superstation, TBS, offered a "Good News" program every evening in 1983. It bombed in the ratings. Only about half the viewers who watched the program preceding it, a rerun of "The Carol Burnett Show," stayed tuned for Turner's cheerful tidings.[4]

Tony Schwartz, author of *Media: The Second God*, says, "People often comment that most of the news we hear today is bad news. The plain truth is that most 'good' news bores us unless it is some highly dramatic development like the discovery of a cure for cancer. News of a bumper wheat crop in the Midwest will make us yawn, but if flood, drought, frost, or tornadoes ruin that crop, we will sit up and take notice."[5]

Consider. What makes a story newsworthy?

Timeliness

News is news when it is new. Fish and news both grow old and spoil in a hurry. Readers, listeners, and viewers want to stay up to the minute. They want to be current with what is happening. Something that occurred last week, or even yesterday, is no longer news. It is history. And reporters leave the writing of history to the historians.

The reporter may include past events to lend perspective to today's news. However, he or she will not keep that job long unless the latest happenings are the focus.

Of Consequence to the Average Person

Each of us has specific interests associated with our work, hobbies, and backgrounds. That is why there are thousands of small and not-so-small publications that target a segment of the population.

Commercial broadcast stations and newspapers, though, are aiming at the interests of the general public. One of their main criteria has to be: How many people want to know about this particular situation? Will this story appeal to a broad range of citizens?

From an Important Source

All of us are interested in knowing what the president of the United States has to say about a certain situation or challenge, especially in times of emergency and severe national problems. We want to hear from the person in charge, the one with the latest and most authentic information.

While reporters periodically will ask the man on the street what he thinks as a human interest angle, the media will try every way possible to get to the top for a definitive reply to their questions.

Of Human Interest

Stories of unusual courage, great sacrifice, outstanding service, and tremendous emotion also pique the interest of the reader, listener, and viewer.

A good example was the story of a tiny child named Jessica McClure who fell into a well in the yard of her Wichita Falls, Texas, home in 1987. We could hear her voice coming from the depths of her dark prison. She became like our own child as we listened across America and identified with the emotions of her anxious, waiting parents.

Suspenseful

Jessica's story was also filled with suspense. Would they be able to get her out in time? Would she die? Why wouldn't they hurry? The entire nation seemed to go on hold as people kept one ear glued to their radios or televisions for the latest report.

Even though some people might not enjoy fictional suspense stories, few can resist being captivated by a story about real people in a dangerous or an unpredictable situation.

The Unusual, the Unique

The very first time something happens, it is newsworthy. After that, it may be done bigger and better by someone else, but it probably will not receive that much attention.

For example, when British athlete Sir Roger Bannister broke the four-minute mile barrier, it made headlines all over the world. Since then, that highly publicized world record has been broken many times. Comparatively little attention has been paid to those who have since run faster and better.

Conflict or Controversy

Get two major forces diametrically opposed to each other in action, and you will have instant news. Nearly all of us—especially Americans—want to know who is going to win. What is the controversy over? What are the facts? It gives us an opportunity to ally ourselves with one side or the other and to anticipate what the final outcome will be.

Author Tony Schwartz says, "In some areas the good news and the bad news come together. This is true of sports, politics and war. These areas involve conflict, winners and losers. News of these conflicts is good news for those who support the winners, and bad news for those who support the losers."[6]

An Explanation of Progress

A developing story keeps our interest. Suspense is built in, especially when we have a great deal at stake in the outcome.

During Operation Desert Storm in 1991, all of us were eager to hear the president or the chief of staff speak in periodic news briefings. We wanted to stay informed about what was happening. Were we winning? How long was the war going to last? Had there been any casualties? It was difficult to pry people away from their television sets for any reason.

Disaster or Tragedy

A natural disaster, such as the volcanic eruption of Mount St. Helens, is a real interest grabber, as is a tragic accident, such as a jet airliner crash. Anything having an impact on the safety and lives of a number of people—or even a few, especially if they are well-known—interests the majority of people.

Proximity to Audience

How close is the reader, listener, or viewer to the story being reported? Will a situation have an impact on the people residing in that coverage area? Do the newsmakers live there or are they well-known in that vicinity? Perhaps they grew up in the area or their parents reside there.

Take a natural disaster, for example. If an earthquake occurs on the other side of the world, we are interested in the overall effect. We may feel sympathy for the people affected, but our attention is short-lived in comparison with a similar disaster that happens in our own country. Then we want more information. We want to know what is being done. Has the president declared it a disaster area? If it is in our own state, or especially our immediate area, coverage will be much more detailed and will continue over a longer period of time.

A national or international story will hold greater interest for the audience of the newspaper, radio station, or television station when a reporter can develop a local slant. People want to know: how will this development or action affect me personally where I live and work? People also are interested in people they know or know of.

Stories of disasters in far-off countries are an exception, but even these may be given a local or personal angle in follow-up stories. For example, a follow-up story on an earthquake in Rumania might find a local angle in covering efforts of local people to raise money for victims, or local physicians traveling to the disaster site to offer medical help.

The fewer people who are interested in an event, the less coverage it receives. For example, a weekly neighborhood newspaper will give space to stories about a local public service club's fundraiser. The article may give the names of the chairmen and committee members, the number of people who attended, the menu, the entertainment for the evening, quotes from a speech, and even a picture of the occasion. An entire page may be devoted to a local school's homecoming event, with pictures of the homecoming queen, the winning touchdown, and a detailed report of the entire event. Most of the readers will have at least a passing interest in the item. A metropolitan daily, on the other hand, has neither the space nor the "majority reader" interest to focus on those types of activities.

Famous People

People are interested in hearing about the rich, the powerful, and the famous.

For example, most people have some kind of pet. Who cares? But think back to the coverage that has been given to the pets of presidents. There were President Roosevelt's dog, Fala; President Nixon's dog, Checkers; and President Johnson's beagle, which got his ears pulled. President Bush's dog, Millie, has even written a book.

There are probably daily incidents of citizens trying to slap or hit a police officer. We do not hear about those occurrences except sometimes when they happen in our own community. But when actress Zsa Zsa Gabor tried her hand at it, it was front page news.

Same Story, Second Verse

News becomes repetitious ... and we know it. More than once and in more than one way, newspapers remind us of deadlines, daylight savings time, tax return day, upcoming elections, governmental services, etc.

The media not only tells us about the coach's resignation — the next day it tells us why; the next it tells us who is named in his place; and the next day it focuses on player protests. Someone who only saw the story on the fourth day would still know the content of the first day's story.

One of the most repeated lines in history is: "... Lee Harvey Oswald, the man the Warren Commission says killed President Kennedy." Is there anyone who doesn't know who Lee Harvey Oswald was? Yes, and there are more of them born every day. Because many of today's adults were living in 1963 and remember Kennedy's assassination, it always seems a waste of time and space to insert a paragraph explaining who Oswald was. Yet there are elementary school students, and perhaps older ones, who would give blank stares at the Oswald name.

What is news? Analyze what is included in the next newscast

you hear or the next newspaper you read. Its coverage is aimed at one thing—capturing the interest of the largest number of readers, viewers, or listeners.

The television networks and local television stations must sell advertising—in the form of commercials—to make their profits and stay in business. (The exception to this, of course, is public broadcasting stations, which are non-profit, supported by viewers and subsidies from corporations, government entities, etc.) Newspapers, for the most part, rely on their advertising sales for their revenues. Subscription costs are a drop in the bucket by comparison. The point here is that advertisers will only advertise in a vehicle that reaches a large proportion of their target market. If the viewers or readers are not watching or reading the substance of the news, those advertising revenues will be lost.

2

Assignments Editor: Architect of the News

Elements of newsmaking: a buzzing, blooming world of particulars. [1]

WILLIAM JAMES

As we read today's newspaper or watch tonight's newscast, it may never occur to us that someone actually planned these news packages in advance. The way most articles are written and reported, they sound as if every item is an "up to the minute" report.

Indeed, many are "late breaking" items, but others — written weeks earlier—are veiled with immediacy by careful use of the present tense:

"Doctors from Miami to Seattle say that the new influenza vaccine ..."

Or with a time-keyed sentence inserted:

"When the sun first hits Lake Michigan tomorrow morning, Larry Perkins will be ..."

Or simply because they are printed or shown on specific dates:

"More than 6,000 youngsters will be darting across Greenville streets with treats in hand tonight, giving little thought to safety precautions ..."

ROLE OF THE ASSIGNMENTS EDITOR

The assignments editor is the person (or team of editors) who schedules coverage by reporters of events or happenings. Although not always called by that name, there is in any news-gathering system—whether a small television station newsroom or a major metropolitan newspaper—a central hub of people whose job is to keep abreast of what is happening in the coverage territory.

It is the assignments editor who assigns a reporter to a murder trial, then calls the courtroom before the trial even begins and re-assigns him to cover the robbery of an armed security car just blocks away. It is this person who is most responsible for what is reported and, thus, for what is read in tomorrow morning's newspaper, heard on a radio newscast, and seen on tonight's news.

The assignments editor dictates the cues to the reporter—the story to cover, the aspect of the situation, and often even the angle to take. Most often the reporter has had an opportunity to read a news release or to call for some background information before being dispatched. However, as in the trial/robbery scenario, there also are many times when he or she is sent scurrying without a notion as to what will be found on arrival at the scene. Nevertheless, it is the reporter's responsibility—and indeed training—to relate accurately to the reader, listener, or viewer what transpired.

While the reporter is the visible member of the team, it is the assignments editor who calls the shots.

PROGRAMMING SOMETHING FOR EVERYONE

In many ways, the individual who serves in the role of assignments editor is as much a programmer as a reporter. The design of the content of an organization's news output is probably most obvious in the television newscast.

The top news story is placed at the beginning of the newscast with a chuckle or light item usually at the end. Inside, of course, are the weather and sports and, sometimes, a business section. Basically, this is the way the average viewer might describe a television newscast.

The assignments editor, however, looks at the newscast as a constantly changing menu designed to entice viewers by offering at least one element that appeals to everyone. He goes through the day as though on a tightrope with a balance pole. When one end of the pole gets a little heavy, he either has to subtract some weight or add to the opposite end.

In case that sounds a little distant, let's take a look at what the editor might face in making assignments for a newscast.

Balancing the News

The perfect newscast is a balance of hard news (natural disasters, legislative entanglements, international conflicts, death, crime, protests, violence, etc.) with soft news (new technology, school dedication, volunteer feature, parade, animal feature, etc.).

Helping to keep the news package symmetrical are local, state, national, and international stories. To this poised scale are added more weights, such as investigative reports versus informational reports and action video versus talking heads and interviews. Surrounding this balancing act are the built-in segments: general news, weather, sports, and business.

This juggling of categories is an effort to assure that there will be something for everyone. Keeping all these variables in mind, the assignments editor tries to assign reporters to cover happenings and interview people, which, when presented as a newscast package, will be balanced proportionately. After all, would anyone want to watch a newscast that was filled with only drug abuse stories or one that contained only feature material?

Stripped down, the thirty-minute newscast is an attempt to appeal to everyone with needed or wanted information—from a farmer wondering about rain in the midst of a drought to a politician hoping his talk on the steps of city hall will be aired; from a tax protester awaiting a verdict on a rollback vote to a young mother who wants to know how to find a good day care center.

When an assignments editor sends a reporter to an event, she may give the reporter background information, tell him what to look for, what angle to take, and how to package the piece into a complete story. In so doing, the editor continues to shape the newscast into a symmetrical presentation.

DATE FILE—SOURCE OF ASSIGNMENTS

But where do the assignments come from? How does the assignments editor know where to send a reporter? Where do the stories originate?

For literally months, the editor has been working on tomorrow's newscast or the newspaper for the next day. As a matter of fact, he often can predict on a Monday a majority of the top news stories to be reported on the following Thursday.

Essential to this operation is a date file. In this file is a folder for every day of the year. Some editors even keep up with dates for coming years. Into this file goes every story idea or notice pertaining to that particular date.

At any time, an editor can pull the file marked February 23 or November 14 and see what has been planned for that date, by whom, the contact person and telephone number, who is involved, and other pertinent information. Some editors categorize the entries by giving them grades of A, B, C, or D, signifying anticipated coverage possibilities; and by type of story, such as political, courts, education, or business.

Sources for Story Information

The sources for stocking a date file are numerous.

News Release. Each day the assignments desk, sometimes operated by more than one editor or even an editing team, receives news releases from businesses, public and private schools, churches, chambers of commerce, shopping malls, governmental departments at every level, civic clubs, military sources, music and arts groups, various societies, support groups, retail stores, social agencies, conventions and fairs, giveaways, and on and on.

The list is limitless. Everyone is hawking something, wanting a photo of a groundbreaking on the front page or a television cameraman to videotape the winner of a shopping cart-filling spree at a grocery store.

Newspaper Clippings. It is a rule of journalism that every news story must contain a time element. When editors read newspapers, magazines, and other publications, they are constantly clipping or making notes of when an event is to occur. It may be a political rally, a protest march, an eclipse of the moon, the first day of horse racing, the last day to register to vote, the opening of a clinic, the closing of a company. Any date that has significance is noted. These, too, are placed in the date file.

Wire Service Reports. The Associated Press, United Press International, and other wire services churn out news items to be used in the future. These are called "advances" and give news organizations the opportunity to plan ahead. They may be written about something as expected as the 400th year anniversary of a historical event or as unexpected as a death. Obituaries of well-known figures are prepared and updated frequently so, in the event of death, the news organization will not be caught trying to scrape together an incomplete biography.

Wire services, through their national and state bureaus, also send their members or subscribers a daily calendar called the "day book." This calendar lists virtually every function, speaker, political gathering, court activity, etc., that has the potential for making an impact on citizens in a particular state or in the entire nation.

Tips from Callers. The call may be from someone who wants publicity for her school, church, or civic club concerning a charitable effort, a speaker, or a special event, and thinks there is merit in reporting it. It may be a parent whose son has attained the rank of Eagle Scout in the Boy Scouts of America and wants the world to know. Most calls of this type are quickly forgotten. However, some are noted and placed in the date file—just in case.

Some tipsters may be angry about what is happening in their neighborhood or about what has happened to them personally. Others think they stand to gain from tipping a news organization about an activity. They might be labeled as whistle blowers, but rarely do they get involved beyond the initial call. Frequently, they do not give their names. But the information—from the dumping of dangerous chemicals in streams to an eyewitness account of a police department payoff—may spark the beginning of an investigative piece of journalism. Many tips do not pan out or they fizzle because the reporter is unable to get more information. But some bring readers or viewers a better insight into their community and society by sparking a cleanup in local industry or exposing an unethical elected official.

Local Calendar of Events. Not unlike the day book dispatched by wire services, most newspapers and larger broadcast operations keep a calendar of events for their own service area. Recorded here is everything from conventions to the annual "Western Days" reunion.

Reporter-Generated Stories. Reporters, particularly those assigned to a regular beat, such as city hall, politics, education, religion, arts, or business, often come across possibilities for stories. They discuss these with the editor and determine if such a story would have merit or appeal.

Follow-Up Items. A follow-up story is one that comes after an original story and gives viewers or readers insight into what has occurred in the meantime. Such stories might include an interview with a fifteen-year-old who was the only survivor of an apartment explosion five years ago, a revisit to a neighborhood devastated ten years ago by a tornado, or a photo essay on how a two-lane farm road grew into an interstate highway during the last twenty years.

Local Angle. The local angle story comes after an original story has been distributed, usually at the national level. If the editor, for example, spots an item in *Newsweek* headlined "Gays Make Inroads into Society," his immediate thought is "What's happening locally in this area?" He may meet with other editors or simply assign a reporter to talk with local activists to develop the local angle to the national story.

All the information gleaned from the various sources and placed in the date files allows the assignments editor to plan his reporters' schedules effectively. There probably will be more ideas than can be used in a month. But none is discarded until after the event. One can never be sure when a minor item may be of benefit.

For example, a convention of dog owners beginning on Friday might not normally merit attention. But if on Thursday there is a national recall of a well-known dog food, then it may have news value for the media and provide "expert" quotes for a local story.

Top Story—First on News

It is no secret that lighter news items are placed at the end of a newscast; the heavy, hard news stories are located at the beginning. In such a format, television news today follows a pattern set years ago by newspapers that handle news similarly—hard news on the front page, first section with lighter fare and features following.

There is, however, a vast difference in broadcast and print news. The newspaper subscriber knows where to locate different categories of news—from sports to comics, from advice columns to television reviews. The reader may grab the sports section first or go immediately to the movie section, but he knows he can go to the front page or any other section at a later time.

Not so with broadcast news. The listener must take each piece of information as it is presented. She can't save something for later.

All of us have returned from an evening out and thought about turning on television to see the news. Then, before reaching for the remote control, we realized the top news stories had already been presented so we did not tune in. After having that experience several times, you may wonder why broadcast program producers continue to follow the hard-to-soft format. Building on the strength of the day's news—starting with features and advancing to the solid top story—would result in fewer viewer dropouts.

Ratings during a newscast would increase rather than decrease.

But even if a producer thought reversing the pyramid would be a good idea, she or he would not dare to vary from hidebound tradition. The fear of alienating viewers, and thus losing ground in the rating game, makes experimentation and innovation too risky.

Network News Evolution: From Headlines to Packages

Television network newscasters during the 1960s and 1970s tried to mention numerous items in their thirty-minute newscasts in order to touch on news of interest to viewers wherever they lived. Immediacy was the key in judging newscasts — "ABC was there first, but NBC had the first pictures."

Then, however, producers began to package their nightly items in bundles of related material. Now a network newscast may contain only eight or ten bundles, but the bundles may contain more than a single item. The makeup of the newscast no longer strives for something immediate from:

- the West Coast (California fires threaten $5 million dollar homes)
- the Midwest (no rain for seven weeks in Iowa)
- the East (sludge washes into Boston Harbor)
- the South (apartment fire in New Orleans kills eight)
- Washington, DC (president signs bill today)
- New York (Wall Street plunge cuts trading)
- plus three international items

Instead, producers now create the basis of their newscast by taking a "national" view of continuing issues—the homeless in winter, the dilemma of the economy, funding for the arts, no place for waste, etc. While there is still an attempt to pull elements from across the nation for a geographical balance and to relate major immediate stories to viewers, locale is more often the producer's call than the story's.

Immediacy of Radio News

When we need truly immediate information, we listen to radio news because it is the fastest mass communications available. Newspapers have to set type and get the printed word out; local television stations are bound to the network programming in such a way that it requires a major effort to interrupt it.

We need to know if it is going to be raining when the kids get out of school; we need to know if there is a traffic jam on our main artery to work; and we need to know if the telephone outage is continuing in our downtown area. Radio can give us this information in our brief drive to the office.

We also complain about radio's litany of headlines. One of the constant complaints of radio listeners is, "Why do you keep repeating the same news hour after hour?" Listeners fail to realize that it is only a repeat if they heard it previously. Otherwise, of course, it is indeed news to them and to others who have just tuned in.

We are drawn to the news media like filings of iron to a magnet. There is a pull in the direction of information, but if the iron is too heavy or if the magnet is too weak, it will not move.

We read, watch, and listen because past experience has proven that we will be attracted by something we did not know that will please or help or affect us in some way—severe weather approaches, the Oakland A's win, the school superintendent resigns, Kevin Costner's new movie opens, the city limits trash pickups.

But if the pull is not great enough or if we are "too heavy" into other things, we—like the filings of iron—will not move.

Financial Considerations—The Bottom Line

When all is said and done, the bottom line in all the decisions made about the evening newscast boils down to a financial consideration. All the stations in a given market are in a never-ending competition with each other for viewers. Every station wants you as a regular viewer. For that reason, they are constantly trying to make their newscast the best, the most attractive and enticing. The winner in viewer ratings has much to gain financially since that station's advertising rates are based on how many people will be watching the commercials. That, of course, translates into the amount of profit for the station.

NBC reporter Linda Ellerbee points out that news is not the most important product in the TV news business. Rather it is the audience, sold at a price to the sponsor. "In television the product is not the program, the product is the audience and the consumer of that product is the advertiser. ... The manufacturer (network) that gets the highest price for its product is the one that produces the most product (audience). ... Altruists do not own television stations or networks, nor do they run them. Businessmen own and run them. Journalists work for businessmen. Journalists get fired and cancelled by businessmen. That is how it is."[2]

Most viewers and those in the news business would agree that there is never a perfect newscast. Although perfection is the goal, the reality is that most newscasts don't work out exactly as desired. Along the way a feature does not pan out. Then, just before air time, an explosion at an antique store pushes itself to the top of the newscast. The result? The evening news has grown top heavy with hard news.

The point remains: without the ever-present attempt to balance the newscast, it would be very lopsided indeed. And it would fail to give the wanted and needed information for the farmer, the politician, the protester, and the young mother.

3

Why Reporters Act that Way

*The journalist's relationship to the world he or she covers is not a
direct one but is mediated by practical concerns: how to report a
world of activities within the constraints of publication deadlines
and news space limitations, how to determine the factual character
of accounts, how to formulate events into a story, and so on.* [1]

MARK FISHMAN, *Manufacturing the News*

The reporter is the person whose byline is placed just above the article you read in the newspaper, or the one you see standing in front of a courtroom door saying, "... for now the jury continues to deliberate. This is Janis Evans, Channel 7 News."

The reporter is your witness at the scene of a flood, the person who questions the district attorney for you, the eyes searching for details of kickbacks in city government, the voice reminding you that there are only eight more shopping days until Christmas, the translator who cuts through hours of political rhetoric and gives you a concise seven-inch story on the metropolitan page.

Because the reporter is there when we cannot be, readers, listeners, and viewers almost instantly begin to trust this stranger. Indeed, they begin to feel that this is someone they know, a friend in whom they can place their confidence.

Most often there is no reason to distrust this person who is invited into the home each night or whose words are read daily at America's breakfast tables. Yet, there are pitfalls that reporters face, pressured moments, deadline constraints, and situations over which they have no control that may skew an otherwise accurate account and may cause them to act much differently than the smiling reporter who is welcomed each evening into thousands of living rooms.

To the source or the target of news stories, the public image and the personal contact with a reporter may seem worlds apart. They may often seem to be almost a different species. But what often appears to the onlooker to be an individual who is harried, hurried, aggressive, and even aggravating will be better understood by comprehending the pressures, the challenges, and the role of the reporter.

REASONS BEHIND THE ACTIONS

The Public's Right to Know

First of all, the reporter represents the public. And the public has a right to know. Most reporters have an extraordinary commitment to keeping the public informed. Many will go to unusual lengths to fulfill what they consider a major obligation of their profession.

Responsibility to Assist the Reporter

If you are a public official of any kind, then you have an obligation to help the reporter get the information needed. This response also will help to ensure that what is reported is factual and free from error. Leaving the reporter to his or her own devices will often result in a less positive report, one that is potentially laden with error or presents only part of the overall picture.

Even if you are not in the role of a public official, you will usually find it to your advantage to cooperate with the reporter. This gives you the opportunity to present your side of the story, your viewpoint.

Accurate, Objective News—Goal of the Reporter

The reporter's job is to give the public accurate, objective news, even when the news is bad. Reporters are not concerned with how the promulgation of a certain set of facts will affect your institution, your business, or you personally. They are interested in making sure that they report factually and accurately—within the parameters of the constraints thrust upon them by the nature of their job.

Watchdogs of Freedom of the Press

Freedom of the press in America has had its champions from

the time of the earliest Colonial publishing efforts. John Peter Zenger, after coming to America from his native Germany in 1710, established *The New York Weekly Journal* in opposition to the Colonial government. Brought to trial on a charge of seditious libel against the provincial governor, Zenger won acquittal, a decision that set the tone for the freedom of the press guaranteed in the Bill of Rights.[2]

Article I of the Bill of Rights states that "Congress shall make no law ... abridging the freedom of speech or of the press ...." Reporters zealously guard this democratic principle. To them, the principle of free access to information takes precedence over any circumstances.

While we may not always appreciate how much freedom the press has, particularly if we or our organization have been covered in a negative way, still the alternative is much worse. As highly respected American journalist Walter Lippman said, "A free press is not a privilege but an organic necessity in a great society."[3] And New York Senator Daniel Patrick Moynihan observed, "If you are traveling around the world and want to know where you are, pick up a newspaper ... If you read a newspaper with good news, you're in a dictatorship; if you see a newspaper filled with bad news, you're in a democracy."[4]

William Harley, a U.S. State Department consultant, told an international gathering:

> A free press serves three major functions. First, it acts as a major source of information, so that people are provided the raw material from which to form opinions and make choices from a wide variety of viewpoints. Second, an unshackled press serves as a monitor, scrutinizing the activities of government and reporting how authority is exercised. Third, a free press serves as a liaison between the state and its citizens. It serves the latter as a sounding board, permitting them openly to voice criticism and complaints as well as suggestions. Through the free press government is continually informed of the people's opinion of its performance.[5]

And as Supreme Court Justice Felix Frankfurter observed, "Freedom of the press, however, is not an end in itself, but a means to the end of a free society."[6]

Censorship—A "Red Flag" Word

Censorship is the most offensive word in the reporter's vocabulary. Using threats or bribes to try to silence a reporter is a foolish and dangerous approach to take. Such tactics will invariably end up in the newspaper and/or a news report at the offender's expense. A recent incident illustrates the negative consequences of such an approach.

Ken Milstead, editor of *The Suburban Tribune*, a Dallas weekly newspaper, called Don Vickery, a local bank president, upon hearing that he had resigned. Vickery told Milstead that he was being replaced by a management representative of a holding company that had signed a letter of intent to buy the bank. He invited the newspaper to attend a farewell party for him. Milstead sent a photographer, but immediately received a call from a bank officer informing him that "any story, picture or cutline had to be read and approved by the bank."

When Milstead responded that he would not allow censorship of his paper, the official insinuated that the paper would lose the bank's advertising if he did not comply, and that it would be in his "best interest" to do as he said.

The next day Milstead called the new bank president about the pending sale of the bank and was told that the bank would issue a news release the following week. When a reporter followed up the next week, the new president was very rude and hung up on her. The editor received the same treatment when he called back. A story about the bank's new attitude made the front page of the

FUNKY WINKERBEAN

newspaper and did anything but enhance the bank's reputation and standing in the community.[7]

Accurate, Balanced Reporting—An Obligation

Reporters have a responsibility to protect the credibility of their station or newspaper by reporting a story accurately — no more, no less. They also are obligated to give a well-balanced report, to present all sides of a controversial situation. Those who are un-cooperative or refuse to be interviewed forfeit the right to present their viewpoint and the facts justifying or backing up their stance or actions. While reporters want to present both sides of a story, they will go with whatever they have in order to meet a deadline.

Pre-Conceived Plan

One of the problems of dealing with a reporter could be a pre-conceived story idea. There are times when a reporter has read a wire story, a newspaper article, or a magazine piece and calls for a comment from an official. The expectation is that the interviewee will respond in the same vein with the same general flavor. When the official cannot substantiate the information or counters it, the reporter is apt to believe something is being hidden.

He may go to great lengths to find another comment to verify the original story simply because he believes he has been led astray or misinformed. The first message heard is the one the reporter (and, indeed, each of us) tends to believe until overwhelming data convinces otherwise. The spokesperson in such a situation must be

Tom Batiuk

more than convincing in order to overcome the inability of the reporter to grasp the truth.

Ever-Present Deadlines

Reporters are in a never-ending race with the clock to meet their daily deadlines. These often limit a reporter's time to make small talk and utilize her social graces. Reporters often appear to be abrupt and pushy because their jobs depend on consistently, day in and day out, getting a story by cutoff time. Finishing a story on time often results in an incomplete, one-sided report unless those involved are helpful and prompt in their responses.

Evasiveness and Misleading Statements— Dangerous Tactics

Reporters get "uptight" if they feel a person is being evasive or is deliberately trying to give a false impression. This approach can often lead to a negative story. It also can result in a suspicious reporter who is determined to get to the bottom of the matter. Even worse, a pattern of this type of response can put the person or organization under the constant scrutiny and watchful eye of the news media, which is now searching for any hint of wrongdoing or subterfuge.

Career Goals of Reporters

Every reporter wants his or her story to end up as the opening report on the evening news or as the major headline, front page ar-

ticle in the morning newspaper. This builds in a constant desire to make each story as exciting, controversial, and eye-opening as possible. Sometimes, as a result, more seems to be made of a particular situation than is actually there.

Reporters' Decisions are Limited

In working with the news media, it is important to understand that reporters do not make all the decisions about a story. Unless a reporter works a regular beat, the assignments editor has, in all likelihood, assigned not only the story to be covered but also the approach to be taken. This may also be true of a certain story a reporter covering a particular beat has been given.

Reporters assigned to a particular beat are also expected to produce a certain amount of copy each day—even when nothing of significance is happening.

Mark Fishman, in his book, *Manufacturing the News*, tells of a study he conducted on beat reporters. He said that, on the average, beat reporters turned in from two to six stories a day. A city hall reporter could recall only two days out of his four years on the beat when he wrote nothing at all. "The obligation to produce news every day was so strong that even when both the city editor and the reporter agreed that nothing was happening on the beat, the reporter was still responsible for writing something about the beat," Fishman says.[8]

Stories will be edited. This is especially true of television and

radio news stories. The reporter may interview you for two or three minutes, but the finished story may contain only twenty seconds of the interview. It may even be boiled down to one sentence or a part of a sentence. Or a newspaper, due to space limitations, may cut what you consider the very heart of an article about you or your business.

Remember that the introduction of the story by the television news anchor can drastically change the impact and tone of the story. What seemed to be a positive, harmless approach by the reporter in the interview can suddenly take a negative turn because of the way it is introduced.

Newspaper headlines are not written by the reporter but by a headline specialist. A headline can develop a negative mindset in the reader's eye for the rest of the story, or it can even slant the whole story.

A television reporter's story may be bumped if something more important, shocking, or frightening happens in the meantime. After all that trouble, your interview may wind up on the cutting room floor.

The world of the reporter is often a pressure pot of deadlines, unrealistic demands, uncooperative people, and tremendous challenges to come up with a great story. Most reporters, however, overcome these demands and are conscientious and professional in their approach and dealings with others.

4

Strategies of the Reporter

*When a San Marcos dictator is shot in Woody Allen's film
Bananas, sportscaster Howard Cosell, in a spoof of the mass media
interviewer, jabs the microphone in the dictator's face and intones,
"When did you first realize it was all over, sir?"* [1]

IRV BROUGHTON, *The Art of Interviewing for Television,
Radio and Film*

There are several features that, through tradition and training, are
critical to reporters. They are essentials to the profession, the fire
that tempers each dispatch. These are forever sought; they are
never satiated: time, facts, contacts, unabashed curiosity, and clear,
concise writing.

Time. Nothing drives a reporter more than the element of
time. It is as much a part of the competitive battle for news as the
story itself. For when a reporter is second with the story, he or she
has lost the edge. A story in a metropolitan newspaper must have
something new—an angle, an emotional appeal, a boldness that
pierces through the fact that a competitor broke the story first.

Facts. Sifting through the rhetoric, reading background, listening to tapes of a meeting, and remembering what was seen at a
retirement party could be just activities for some, but for a good
reporter who has learned to put loose parts of a puzzle together,
they are much more. Knowing what to pull out of memory and
what is irrelevant are marks of experience.

Contacts. It takes only a little reporting to know that once
good information has been obtained from an individual, he or she
also might provide quotes, insight, comments, or direction for a future story. Touching base with these individuals on a somewhat

regular basis builds a mutual trust and can produce additional story possibilities.

Unabashed Curiosity. Some people think news reporters are born with a brash, persistent mind for interrogation. But the truth is that anyone who works as a reporter quickly learns that the way to get people to talk—and thus get their story—is to ask questions. Sometimes reporters direct the questioning beyond polite curiosity. They cut right to the heart of the matter—and to the heart of the interviewee. But, oftentimes, they do get the story.

Clear, Succinct Writing. Another characteristic that comes with the journalist's territory is the necessity to write any story, from a medical research item to a political upheaval, in such a way that it has clear meaning for all. Even though the researcher and the politician may be able to relate to their peers, they frequently lack the ability to explain to an outsider what has taken place.

A HINT OF DECEPTION

Taking these elements into account, one can begin to understand some of the clever ruses a reporter uses to reveal to readers and viewers what has happened in their world.

While the reporter relies on and anticipates the five points outlined above in doing his or her job, each in its own way is also a reporter's adversary. Aside from technical problems, such as getting a satellite link in time for a newscast, and detail problems, such as the correct spelling of a name, simply acquiring the needed information is the toughest part of a reporter's job. No other profession in the world requires such a person-to-person, day-after-day question and answer exchange of information.

An interesting point is that generally interviewees are more than willing to talk with these strangers who represent the mass media. The resulting interchange is sometimes equivalent to two con men trying to outwit each other in sparring with information—hiding it, altering it, and giving it piecemeal. That is why the reporter depends on strategies such as the following.

Convincing the interviewee that the reporter has most of the information already. An experienced reporter does his research. He may know that the government agent will not simply tell all. But if he can convince "Mr. Big Agent" that he already knows what happened in a fatal insecticide spraying incident and just needs to tie up some loose ends, Mr. Big begins to fill in first names, a time of day, the type of crop plane used, and often even more than the reporter dared hope for. In so doing, he also drops more details of the original story, which the reporter needs. The reporter continues the patter and persuasion until he has the nugget he was searching for. Then, new information in hand, he goes to his next interview candidate, better armed than before. And so it goes until the complete insecticide death story is developed.

Using the "we'd like to give you some publicity" line. No news organization is in the business of providing publicity. Often, publicity comes about as a result of news stories, but it is a by-product. Publicity is a word popularized by advertising and promotion people. Consequently, when a news reporter uses the term, it conjures up thoughts of free advertising and positive coverage for an organization. The positive or negative merits of the interview, however, will not be known by the interviewee until the story is published.

Intimidating the interviewee. "Mr. Allen, my story is going to run tomorrow regardless of whether you comment on it. Your employees have spoken, and I just think the president of the company should have the opportunity to explain his side of this issue." Depending on the situation and how Mr. Allen fits into it, that sort of tactic may elicit a comment. While it is not a threat, Mr. Allen may feel threatened by the unknown remarks of his employees and decide to talk.

Using an assumed name and a facade of naiveté. Have you ever called a store or business and wanted to remain anonymous? "Er, just checking on your price for a lawn mower, model 57J-62," you might say. Maybe you have already called twice previously and failed to write the price down, or perhaps you know the owner and do not want him thinking you would go elsewhere to buy. Whatever the reason, sometimes we want to pretend we are just plain John Doe.

That is the basis of another reporter tactic. By calling not as a reporter but as a customer or an interested visitor to the city or a first-grade teacher, sometimes the person on the other end opens up freely with information. Names, telephone numbers, street addresses, spouse's name, etc., sometimes are divulged easily from "neighborly folks," when they are unaware they are talking with the news media.

ABC-TV's "Prime Time Live" used this ploy in a 1991 investigative report on tele-evangelists. Posing as representatives of a ministry interested in contributing to orphans in Haiti, they coaxed an orphanage operator into "spilling the beans" about how he provides income tax dodges for contributors. Of course, he had no idea he was being videotaped. Some of his remarks were incriminating not only to the person the program was investigating but also to him. What he was tricked into saying was, no doubt, of interest to Internal Revenue Service officials. Later he tried to deny what he had said, but the videotape was difficult to refute.

Reporters at WFAA-TV in Dallas, the area's dominant news station, have on more than one occasion used a ploy in getting quick information about an airport crisis. By calling the airport, saying they are from 'FAA (a shortened version of their call letters, but also the abbreviation for the Federal Aviation Administration) and need to know what is happening, they have gotten swift answers.

Presenting an opportunity to give your side of the story. "This is Jerry Cole with Channel 3. We know the media have been giving a lot of misinformation about your railroad the past few days, and we think you deserve to tell your side of the Idaho Avenue intersection problem. I would like to just sit down with you and spend some time hearing about some of the problems you are facing."

Getting on the right side of the railway manager, convincing him that the reporter is on his side and not aligned with those other dastardly journalists who have been bashing the railroad for holding up traffic at an intersection is the idea. It could be, of course, that the other side is told; or it could be that the reporter wants inside information about the situation. At any rate, an offer to counter the negative stories of other news outlets may get a reporter closer to the principal player and closer to the truth.

Offering to go "off the record." Reporters seeking information and getting rebuffed may offer an "off the record" opportunity for prospective interviewees. This, of course, means the journalist wants to talk about a story, but vows not to disclose the contents of the conversation. Few reporters would go against the ethics of an "off the record" interview. Some have even spent time in jail holding to their promise not to disclose a source.

The up-side of such an interview for the journalist is that he or she can take the information, find others who will verify what was learned, then quote from or allude to a second informant.

A study conducted by a Bowling Green University professor found that whether the news story had no attribution, general attribution, or specific attribution did not make a substantial difference in reader perceptions. He suggests that journalists could reduce or even omit much of the attribution in news stories without affecting their credibility with readers. Regardless of how the reporter got the information or to whom it is attributed, the coverage can be just as damaging.[2]

Erwin Knoll, editor of *The Progressive*, presents another facet of the "off the record" interview. He maintains that today "off the record" usually translates to "Feel free to use this information and even my words, but don't let anyone know I'm the one who told you." He says, "Obviously, a reporter who enters into such an agreement of confidentiality can subject the reading, viewing, or listening public to outrageous abuse. Freed from accountability for their words, news sources can palm off falsehoods and distortions without fear of effective challenge."[3]

Then there are variations on "off the record." "On background" means that the journalist cannot quote the source by name but can use the information and attribute it to an unnamed spokesperson such as "a high government official." When Henry Kissinger was Secretary of State, he sometimes had reporters credit his remarks to "a senior official on the Secretary of State's plane."[4]

"On deep background" indicates that the information can be used but the reporter must act as though he got it from the air. Officials also have been known to use phrases to inform or influence a reporter without having to take any direct responsibility. A couple of examples are: "I wouldn't steer you away from that," and "If you looked into it and asked the right questions, you just might find something interesting."[5]

Phrasing of questions. Journalists know that the way they phrase a question commands a like response. It is a gimmick similar to the old "When did you stop beating your wife?" question. No matter how you answer, you are automatically guilty.

Because editing of videotape or the article is done later, a juxtaposition of the order of the answers can be made, some can be left out entirely, and the writing that is placed before and after the quotes can be slanted. Agreeing to an interview makes you vulnerable to the whims of the reporter. The interviewee will not see the story before it is printed or have any input into the editing of the evening news story. The snippets of the interview finally used in the story may even belie the persuasion of the interviewee.

Clinging to a preconceived idea. There are times when a reporter has already decided what happened or what is about to happen. Whether her thinking has been programmed by the assignments editor or a morning newspaper article, a reporter may be convinced that the election of a new association president is the result of the ousting of the current president, who has been criticized for overspending. Although no one can be found to substantiate the preconceived idea, an inexperienced reporter may resort to creative writing simply to sustain the idea in the article. She also may use only the information that will back up her opinion and leave out any facts that would refute her preconceived opinion.

Using the guise of doing a positive interview. A reporter will sometimes make it appear that the story is going to be very positive. In fact, the interview may start on a congratulatory note. Suddenly, though, the tone will change drastically with the reporter trying to put the interviewee on the spot. Perhaps the reporter has a document or some kind of record the interviewee does not know about, or someone has accused the person of fraud. In a television interview when the switch comes, the videographer will be sure to have a tight closeup of the interviewee's shocked or embarrassed expression.

For example, a school principal might be asked for an interview about standardized test scores that have gone up significantly in that school over the previous year. The reporter may begin with plaudits for the school and the principal, but suddenly begin to grill the interviewee about a tip the station received that teachers had been teaching the test for weeks before it was given.

Assuming a watchdog role. A reporter whose suspicion is aroused or whose belief is that he has not been treated fairly may decide to scrutinize a politician, an agency, or an industry in hopes of finding something negative to report. A reporter's "bad list" is not a good place to be.

There is no question that these and other strategies are used daily by members of the mass media in developing news stories. But that is not to say there is intent to defraud the public. The conscientious journalist's aim is truth and openness.

ETHICAL APPROACH OF MEDIUM

However, when you get into the realm of "yellow journalism," sensational rags, and scandal sheets, no device is too devious. Next time you are waiting in the supermarket line, thumb through the *National Enquirer, Globe,* or the *World.* These publications have to depend on their covers' shock value to get buyers and pay their bills. "Fixing" a photo with a head of a person from one picture and a body of an animal from another picture, out and out fabrications, and extreme distortions of events in the lives of the rich and famous are only a few of their imaginative approaches.

Consumers of the news definitely need to know the ethical stance and viewpoint of a particular medium in evaluating what they see and hear.

But even in the "legitimate" media, the way some people are ridiculed and intimidated, one wonders why anyone whose persona is tainted by rumors or misdeeds would permit news reporters to invade his private life by agreeing to an interview.

One answer may be found in the fact that these men and women have managed for years to overcome other human competitions, such as peers fighting for the same company promotion or raise, thwarting any encroachment on their position. They are accustomed to confrontations and to winning. They like the challenge. They see themselves as invincible and, consequently, are eager for a good "televised" bout.

Mike Wallace, network television's first confrontational interviewer, once said interviewees respect the fact that they are going to have a large television audience, that they are going to have the opportunity to get their point of view across to the American public and believe that, unless there is something to hide, there is no reason not to do the interview.[6]

Fascination with the media is part of the ploy, too. Wallace said his "CBS Reports" staff once begged for only a few minutes of interview time with an individual. After much negotiation, they received an okay for just a few minutes. But when the prescribed time was up, the interviewee willingly agreed to extend the time to whatever length was asked.[7]

It does not take much on-the-job experience for a reporter to learn to capitalize on the human being's natural desire for recognition and attention in getting the story he is after. The reporter soon becomes adept in the psychology of flattery, intimidation, threats, promises, or whatever else it takes to get a particular interviewee to talk and cooperate. Whether the end result resembles what the interviewee had in mind ... well, that's often a different story.

5

Cultivating Good Rapport with the News Media

People are too savvy ... the internal grapevine is too active ... news media are too investigative for an ... organization to get around to communicating whenever management feels there's something they want somebody to know. [1]

LYNDA STEWART, former president of International Association of Business Communicators

Developing an ongoing, good working relationship with media representatives—particularly reporters and assignments editors—is the best guarantee for sensitive, fair, and accurate handling of news affecting you and your organization. This means taking the time and effort to learn about the needs and operation of the particular news media that cover your area of endeavor.

- What is their mode of operation?
- When are their deadlines?
- What are they interested in?
- Who are the reporters and assignments editors in various news areas?
- Whom is the newspaper owned by or affiliated with?
- What is the station's network affiliation?
- Who owns the station and what are their political leanings?
- What can you congratulate them for? An award a reporter has won? A ratings increase for their station?

WHAT THE PROS SAY

A recent panel, composed of assignments editors from radio stations, gave some helpful tips.

- Be sure to send information to the current person, not one who left the station a year ago.
- Find out if you are addressing a man or a woman named Kelly (or whatever) and make certain you are spelling the name correctly.
- Add a personal touch. This could be a handwritten greeting at the bottom of a news release or a note about how this story would appeal in a special way to that particular station's listeners or newspaper's readers. One editor mentioned that he always picks out the hand-addressed envelopes from the mountain of information he receives and opens those first.
- Be familiar with the station's format and targeted listening audience.[2]

WAYS TO GET AND KEEP NEWS
MEDIA CONFIDENCE

If you function in the role of a spokesperson or news contact person for a group or an organization, there are some definite things you should remember in order to keep in the good graces of media people.

Get to know reporters and news assignment editors personally, on a first-name basis. Become acquainted with their individual interests and manner of operating.

Release all stories to all the media at the same time. You must be as neutral as Switzerland in this regard. You cannot afford to play favorites. While you may try to curry favor with the one or few to whom you give an "inside tip" or an early news release, the irritation or even wrath of those left out can have serious and long-lasting repercussions. You may find that your stories in the future are either overlooked or reported from a negative point of view.

However, if a reporter comes to you looking for an idea for a feature story, that is a different matter. Once you suggest a possibility and the reporter expresses interest in it, you should not give the idea to someone else unless you are certain the first one has no intention of pursuing it.

Respect the inevitable competition among reporters and the media they represent. Don't tip one reporter off about a story another reporter is working on.

Always return calls from the news media promptly. Let them know that they can depend on you for an immediate response to their questions and that you understand their role and responsibility.

Respect a reporter's deadlines. Call during deadline time *only* in an emergency. Release fast-breaking news mid-morning, if possible, which will usually allow reporters to meet deadlines.

Keep in mind the different interests of radio, television, daily newspapers, and weekly newspapers in the information you send out and in responding to queries from various reporters.

News media conferences should be called only for the release of very important topics. These should be brief and should focus on one area of information only. Calling conferences for what the media would consider trivial purposes will result in either low attendance or non-attendance.

Be meticulous in the accuracy of the information you release. A few mistakes on your part will quickly earn you the reputation of an unreliable source—a designation that is difficult to overcome. Being honest and candid equals credibility, and credibility is absolutely essential in order to deal effectively with the news media.

Craig Gifford, while serving as deputy executive vice president of the Ohio School Boards Association, said, "I think the real barometer of an effective relationship is if the media regularly and routinely depends on you as the source of all stories. When they start checking behind your back, you are apparently not dealing effectively with them."[3]

Make sure reporters know how to contact you after hours and that they have your correct phone number.

Stay on top of national news in your area of operation. Local reporters may not always be aware of the bigger picture. You can make your organization look better by drawing parallels with such information, and you also can help make the reporter look better by assisting him or her in including valid comparisons and statistics in a story.

Say "thanks" for a job well done. A phone call or, even better, a note to the reporter with a copy to the reporter's boss is a nice touch and may give you an opportunity to plant a seed for a future positive story.

Be sure to let the news media know if a scheduled event has been called off.

If an incident happens that could have a negative effect on your organization, it is better for you to inform the news media up front rather than to wait and have them ferret out the story. Lining up people involved (after notifying them) with whom reporters can talk, preparing background information, issuing a statement of concern and what is being done to rectify the problem can go a long way toward lessening the impact of a potentially derogatory report. That kind of active response also can be effective in building credibility with the news media.

As one reporter said: "When are administrators going to realize that if we don't get the negative news from them, we're going to get it from someone? Then it may be secondhand, inaccurate or totally out of proportion. Administrators want us to gloss over or ignore unfavorable news, then to stand in line for an interview about all of the good things they have to report."[4]

Save complaints and criticisms for serious problems. Minor errors are inevitable; however, constant clamoring will destroy an effective working relationship. Even when the error is serious, discuss the problem with the involved reporter. Complaints to the editor should be made only if an issue cannot be resolved with the reporter.

Maintain a file of photos and updated biographies of all top people in your organization.

WHEN YOU ARE BEING INTERVIEWED

Once you have agreed to be interviewed for a story, here are some important things to remember.

Respect the reporter's deadline. If necessary, readjust your own schedule to conform to the needs of getting the report in on time. Return all calls promptly.

Give the reporter the facts—straight, honestly, and sincerely. Reporters seem to have a sixth sense that tells them when someone is trying to mislead them or distort the truth. If you don't know for sure, don't guess. Offer to find out and get back with them.

Make sure the reporter fully understands the situation. This is your best protection against outright errors in a story or a misleading slant. This is especially important if a reporter is a newcomer to your town or has just been assigned to a beat covering your area. He may not know enough of the background to report accurately and, with ever-present deadlines hanging over him, may not have time to find out.

Be helpful to the reporter, but never try to dictate how the story should be reported. That is strictly the reporter's responsibility and prerogative—one she carefully guards.

Don't ask to see or hear a story before it is used. There is no way a reporter will agree to getting your approval. An exception might be if the interview involves highly technical material. Then you might tactfully offer to check the story for accuracy ... if the reporter would like.

Make your staff and facilities available. Line up other people the reporter might wish to interview. Have an open door policy to the extent that is possible within the parameters of confines such as security and confidentiality.

Be helpful without seeming to guard the reporter. If the reporter is going to interview someone else, provide background information, escort her to the scene, but don't hover over her. Otherwise, you may unwittingly give the appearance of having something you don't want the reporter to see or know about.

Give advance notice of a newsworthy event. Be sure to notify assignments editors and reporters in plenty of time to get it worked into their schedules. If something exciting comes up at the last minute, by all means call reporters. Who knows? It may be a slow news day. They may just be sitting around waiting for a good story to pop up.

Respect the reporter's role, but don't stand in awe of it. When we see a reporter frequently on the evening news, he may seem to become larger than life. Really, though, reporters are just ordinary people trying to do a demanding job.

Be brief without being curt. This applies whether it is writing a news release, contacting the assignments editor or reporter by phone, or during a formal interview. Whoever you are talking to will appreciate your getting to the point without his having to weed through some long-winded discourse to figure out what on earth you are trying to say.

One reporter expressed his frustration in dealing with school people in this way: "Educators drone on and on. It's all I can do to get two or three usable, concrete thoughts out of an hour-long interview or a five-page letter. They never really say anything."[5]

Learn from the reporter. The reporter knows a lot about public opinion and what is going on in the community that may be valuable to you in your particular area of responsibility.

Analyze stories for possible constructive criticism. You may not like the way the story came out, but ask yourself, "What can I learn from it?" Is there something that can be improved in your organization that the story highlighted, or next time can you be more effective in the way you field questions?

Cultivating good rapport with the news media does not just happen. It takes time and an ongoing commitment to building and keeping an open and productive relationship. But it is well worth the effort. As James E. Lashley, a former newsman turned public relations professional, put it, "Don't get on his back; scratch it. He may do the same for you."[6]

6

Getting Your Message Out

What the unabashed self-promoter does is to play with his material to see which slant is most appropriate for the media source he is approaching. The most appropriate approach has everything to do with what the source sees as its mission and its audience and how your material and your angle square with them. [1]

DR. JEFFREY LANT, *The Unabashed Self-Promoter's Guide*

Your angle may be to get favorable publicity for your organization, your business, or yourself. But the news media are not in the publicity-giving business; they are looking for news. In order to fulfill your purpose, you must show them the newsworthy angle in your activities, accomplishments, goals, and projects. Telling a reporter or editor that you want "some publicity" is a surefire interest killer —even if your story does have merit from a news standpoint.

WHICH MEDIUM SHOULD GET WHICH MESSAGE?

Which of the media would be interested in covering your story? Getting your message before the public requires some homework on your part. Study the news media and notice the types of stories they use. What audience does a certain medium reach? What is its coverage area?

A big city daily newspaper's goal is to reach the total population in that city and the surrounding smaller towns. It also will likely have a state edition, which appeals to an even wider readership. It is not likely to use a story about your local high school's homecoming queen unless there is a very unusual aspect, such as the election of a blind girl or a boy.

However, a close perusal of the dailies reveals specialized interest columns and pages and various calendars, which may very well give you a forum. Most dailies have columnists who write on pursuits and concerns of special ethnic, age, hobby, or community groups. For example, take the activities of a church. Your religious group's concert will not make the front page, but it probably would rate a small blurb in an activities column on the Saturday religion page. The same information also might be used in the arts section or an entertainment guide, especially if the group is well known. An item about a seminar on managing finances could find a home in the business section or on an events calendar if the general public is invited. A youth group that adopts nursing home residents as "grandparents" might make a feature story in a daily's living section.

Find out the names of the editors or columnists who will likely be interested in the types of stories you want to see in print. Address your news release to those specific journalists by name. Do not assume that the appropriate person will get your information if you just send it to the newspaper.

Another way to interest an urban newspaper in your story is to get a well-known person involved in your activity in some way. The activity itself may not be deemed of widespread interest, but the personality may be. For example, the Dallas Independent School District planned to dedicate a mobile homemaking unit, which would visit low-income families and teach adults homemaking and parenting skills. While the program was obviously worthwhile and innovative, it was hardly a front page story. However, when the new Dallas mayor's wife agreed to cut the ribbon, the importance of the item was upgraded. The result was that stories were run by the three major television stations on the evening news, and accounts of the event with a picture were in both daily newspapers the following day.

The weekly newspaper in a city and the community newspaper that publishes once or twice a week in a smaller town have quite a different purpose than the metropolitan newspaper. They are interested in covering news about the people and events in their own community. They welcome stories that the big city press would turn up its nose at.

There is also the distinct possibility that your story will have a greater impact on those you want to reach in your community

newspaper than in the urban publication. It will almost certainly receive more space so that more details can be included.

Kathie Magers, editor of *The Oak Cliff Tribune,* a Dallas weekly, says, "Unlike the metro papers, we are not only willing, but enthusiastic about printing news of local events and local people ... that means everything that happens in our circulation area."[2] A local high school graduate receiving a college degree or a young person going into the service is considered newsworthy.

Smaller newspapers are usually short on staff and long on work. A well-written news release that can be used with little editing is a welcome sight to most editors. Magers says, "We ask that everything be in writing. Please don't ask that we take it over the phone. We don't have the time, and it's too easy to make mistakes that way."[3] A professional quality picture illustrating your story also will be appreciated and will give you a better chance of being published.

Broadcast Media

In general, stories for radio and television must have the same elements that a daily newspaper requires. It is important, though, to keep in mind the nature of the medium. A newspaper uses the written word and maybe a picture to tell its story. Television depends a great deal on visuals and movement, coupled with verbal description. Its main asset is that it can show and tell. Obviously, action and visual appeal play a big part in a particular activity being selected for a TV story. While television, of necessity, uses "talking heads," a story in which someone can be shown doing something unusual and interesting will be given preference if the two are equal in newsworthiness.

Radio relies solely on sound. Events that have strong auditory appeal and help a listener imagine a happening in his "mind's eye" are naturals for a brief spot on the news. Dan Potter, news assignments editor for Fort Worth's WBAP radio, recommends looking for stories with potential for sound. "Radio has its own style stories," he observes, adding that pointing out how your story can fit its style will give you a much better chance of filling the air waves with what you want to say.[4]

Also, while most television stations are trying to appeal to the masses with their news reports, radio stations usually have a more specialized audience. Many stations focus on a certain ethnic group, a particular age segment, or a specific socioeconomic cluster as their targeted listeners.

By putting a slightly different slant on the same story, you may very well give it appeal for widely varying stations and newspapers. It is certainly worth the time and effort to individualize a story to meet the various media's needs and interests when the end result is more coverage.

Use the News Medium Information form at the end of the chapter to record and file up-to-date information on the news media in your area. Fill out a form for each news medium and keep the forms in a notebook. Be sure to update them regularly.

WHERE CAN YOU FIND IDEAS FOR STORIES?

"Everywhere" is the best answer. Try these for idea-kickers.

- Ground breaking for a new building
- Major executive changes
- Announcement of an important new community service project
- An exhibition or a special show
- Dedication and formal opening of new facilities
- An outstanding acquisition, such as rare books
- A new product
- A significant anniversary
- A visiting dignitary or celebrity
- Award winners
- A member or an employee with an unusual hobby
- A member or an employee who is an outstanding community volunteer
- Honors
- Retirements
- Major speeches and articles
- Deaths
- Significant contribution to a community project or charity
- Publication of a book
- Patents or inventions
- Youth-related activities
- Sporting events
- Cultural events
- Moving to a new location
- Open houses
- Beautification projects

- Environmental protection methods
- Laying a cornerstone

And the list could go on and on.

WHEN SHOULD YOU SUBMIT A STORY?

Keep in mind that news is a highly perishable commodity. News releases should be sent out at least a week before an event happens. Often deadlines require an earlier time frame. Here again, it pays to find out the workings of particular media and editors. For instance, getting an item on a community calendar may require the editor's receiving your release the Wednesday before it is published on Thursday of the following week. Taking into account a leeway for mail delivery, you would probably want to mail to that particular editor about two weeks in advance.

If something unexpected and interesting happens, let Ma Bell help you. Call a reporter with a last-minute tip. She may be hoping the phone will ring on a slow news day.

In addition to formal news releases, send the media copies of newsletters, notices of special events, annual reports, and information about annual meetings and employee recognition. It is amazing what a reporter sometimes will see, in what seems to be an unimportant item, to turn into a feature story.

HOW DO YOU PREPARE A STORY?

Here are some general guidelines to assist you in preparing a professional-looking news release.

Type it, double-spaced, one side only, on 8½ X 11 inch paper. Leave ample margins of about 1½ inches. If you do not have special news release stationery or company letterhead, put your return address in the upper left-hand corner. Line space down three or four times and center the word NEWS RELEASE in caps or boldface type. Skip a couple of spaces and put "Contact:" to the right with the name and phone number of the person the media should call for more information.

At the left, put "For release" with the date it may be used. Skip a space and put a headline, containing a subject and an infinitive or present-tense verb, in caps. Your headline probably will not be used, but it gives the editor an immediate grasp of what your story is about.

Double space and begin your story. If your story must run more than one page, type "More" at the bottom of the page. Then at the top of the next page, put "1st add xxxx" followed by the headline in caps.

End each page with a complete paragraph.

Type "30" or "###" in the center of the page under the final paragraph.

Be sure to keep a copy for your own files.

There is a sample news release at the end of the chapter.

WHAT SHOULD YOU INCLUDE?

Try these suggestions for writing a news release that sounds smooth and professional.

- Include the five w's—who, why, what, when, where—and also tell how. However, don't try to include all this information in the first sentence or even, necessarily, in the first paragraph. Pick out the most vital w's and feature those first. You can include the others later.
- Decide what is most important and interest-piquing about your story and include it in the lead or first paragraph.
- Give your story a personal touch. For example, tell about one particular person who was helped.
- Place the most important information toward the first part of your news release.

- Be accurate and objective. Avoid opinionated statements and adjectives. If you want to say that, for example, the program was excellent, quote a participant who actually said that it was. Keep opinions locked up in quotation marks.
- Use short sentences and words found in everyday conversation. Use strong, colorful verbs.
- Avoid jargon related to your particular field or interest and acronyms that are not spelled out.
- Include full names and identifying titles.
- Be as brief as possible but be sure to cover the important facts about the event.
- List the date, along with the day of the week of an event.

Remember! An editor can learn to rely on you as a dependable and discriminating news source by using the material you prepare, or he can fire you as a reporter by tossing your story in the wastebasket.

WHAT ABOUT PICTURES?

With the exception of "mug" shots, daily newspapers take nearly all their own photos. Weekly newspapers are usually delighted to receive good quality, clear prints to go with a story. Follow these guidelines:

- Submit glossy black-and-white prints at least 5 X 7 in size or a good quality, black-and-white Polaroid® print with plenty of contrast.

- Be sure to identify the people as they appear in the photograph from left to right and tell what they are doing or what they did.
- Never write on the back of the picture or attach anything with a paper clip. Tape your caption to the back of the photo.
- Unless it is a portrait, have the subjects do something more attention-getting than staring at the camera. An informal group is more interesting than a lineup. Editor Kathie Magers says: "... try to get people doing something, if possible, rather than standing in a straight line, and don't take more than five or six in one shot."[5]
- Closeups of faces are more interesting and more attention-getting than full-length long shots.
- If you want a picture returned, write a note to that effect and enclose a self-addressed, stamped envelope. Most often it will be returned, but don't bank on it, especially if it is a one-of-a-kind, irreplaceable shot.

HOW ABOUT A PUBLIC SERVICE ANNOUNCEMENT?

If you have a special event coming up that would be of interest to the general public, try the public service announcement (PSA). Announcements should be sent to a radio station to the attention of the public service director at least three weeks prior to the date of the special event.

Your public service announcement should follow these guidelines (see sample public service announcement at the end of the chapter):

Put your return address in the top left-hand corner. Center and type "Public Service Announcement" underlined or boldfaced. Double space and type: "Contact:", followed by the person's name and phone number in case there are questions. Announcements should be double-spaced.

Put "For use:" with beginning and ending dates that you want the announcement to run.

Include three lengths: a 10-second version, a 15-second version, and a 30-second version.

The length used will, of course, depend on the time available. January through April is a slower time for commercials, so your longer version has a better chance for use during those months.

Television stations also use public service announcements. Since requirements for visual material vary from station to station, contact the public service director for information about his or her particular needs.

FIND OUT ABOUT COMMUNITY BULLETIN BOARDS

Many radio stations, some television stations, and public access cable television channels have community bulletin boards you can use to help publicize a coming event of interest to the community. Such announcements should be typed and sent to the appropriate person at each station at least three weeks in advance. Be sure to include the name and phone number of the contact person in case more information is needed.

PLANNING A NEWS CONFERENCE

A news conference can be very effective in getting out your message when it is used wisely for the right occasion and is put together well. It is appropriate to call a news conference when:

- An event has happened that is of importance to a lot of people.
- A briefing to update developments in a continuing story is appropriate.
- A well-known expert or celebrity is in town briefly.
- A notable announcement is to be made.

Calling a news conference for a trivial reason will rapidly turn into a non-event with little or no response. Trying to blow out of proportion the importance of information to be released at a news conference in order to get reporters to attend will ruin credibility with them and their editors. Make sure you have something to share that is important, timely, and of genuine worth. Here are some guidelines to follow in setting up a news conference.

Don't refer to the event as a "press conference." This term not only dates you, it also irritates radio and television professionals who have nothing to do with presses. Use "news conference" or "media conference" instead.

Carefully develop your list of journalists to invite. Make sure your announcement pertains to their areas of interest.

If time permits, send a written invitation even if it must be hand delivered. Follow up with a phone call to help determine an approximate number of attendees. In the case of a late-breaking news conference, invite reporters by telephone.

Set the time for their convenience. Usually a mid-morning conference is best since it gives reporters time to file their stories by deadline.

Notify United Press International (UPI) and Associated Press (AP) Day Book editors about the conference well in advance, if possible.

Don't leak information. It is not only unfair to those attending, but such a tactic will land you in their bad books. Make information available to reporters who are unable to attend after the conference is over.

Select a facility of appropriate size. One too large makes it seem as though few people were interested—even when there is a relatively good turnout. On the other hand, a crowded room is not only irritating to reporters and television crews, but can hamper their getting the best possible story.

Make sure there are enough telephones available, and be certain you can accommodate television needs with heavy-duty extension cords and electrical outlets. Also provide a raised platform or sturdy tables at the back of the room for camera operators.

Display your organization's logo on the front of the lectern or behind the speaker.

Anticipate every possible question and go over them with those who will be interviewed.

Make certain that any audiovisual aids and equipment are in place, working properly, and that their use has been mastered by the person or persons making the presentation.

Prepare a news kit to hand out to reporters. This should include items such as:

- Background information
- A picture of the person named president, the architect of the new building, or whatever is appropriate
- Any pertinent drawings or diagrams
- A copy of the formal statement that will be given at the news conference

- A copy of any audio or video demonstration tape that will be used during the conference

The Day of the News Conference

Have someone posted at the door to greet reporters, pass out news kits, and assist them in any way possible. Provide refreshments—coffee, tea, soft drinks, mineral water, pastries.

The news conference should begin with an introduction of the chief executive officer, celebrity, or other key person. The formal statement would then be given and followed with an opportunity for reporters to ask questions of that person and perhaps a panel of experts, when appropriate.

If an important aspect of the program has not been covered, ask an appropriate question yourself. Or if you are the person being questioned, say something like, "I am often asked ..." Then proceed to answer the question you have raised.

Give the media adequate rein, but do not let the conference get off course. If the subject has been well explored and interest seems to be waning, state, "We have time for one or two more questions."

Thank the reporters for their time and attendance and end the conference.

MAKING NEWS HAPPEN

So far we have talked about getting coverage for things that are happening. But there are activities you and/or your organization can sponsor with the view to enhancing your image and getting news coverage.

For example, Minyard's Food Stores, a Dallas-based grocery chain, sponsors a weekly teacher recognition program. The selected teacher receives a cash award of $1,000, and the student who nominates him or her receives an additional $1,000 for the teacher's school. The effort not only rewards good teaching, it also results in favorable attention and publicity for the sponsor.

Steven Maxx Salon in Dallas decided to pamper two teachers who had lost their jobs due to program cuts in their school system. They offered them a "total day of beauty," which included complimentary haircuts, hair color and makeovers, lunch, manicures, and massages. Not only was it a nice thing to do, it also resulted in a

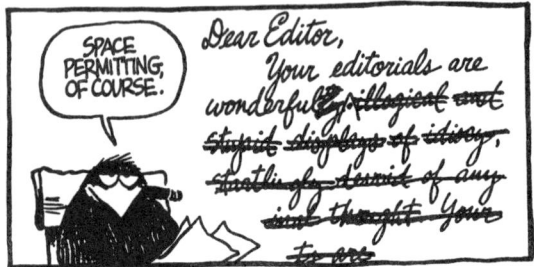

very nice story for the salon in a metropolitan daily. Mentioned were the location of the salon and the fact that it is also a makeover and photography center.[6]

Other possibilities are sponsorship of some type of community benefit, a contest for students, adoption of an inner city school, or a community beautification project.

WRITE AN ARTICLE YOURSELF

Don't overlook the op-ed (opinion-editorial) page, often found just opposite the main editorial page in your metropolitan newspaper. Editors are always on the lookout for well-written pieces that present a specialized viewpoint. Some pay, some don't. But such a piece can help establish you as an authority on a particular subject and present an excellent forum for your own and your organization's messages and opinions.

A letter to the editor is usually easier to get published than an op-ed piece. It, too, will broaden your area of influence and give you an opportunity to refute a misconception or to sway readers' opinions. A letter to the editor should be written very concisely, should focus on only one topic, and should be of interest to the general public.

There are other opportunities in various sections of the newspaper to submit articles of the feature type, which can be used whenever a slot is open that needs filling. This is especially true if you have established yourself as an authority on a particular subject or if you can develop an original, fresh angle.

Of course, there are many other outlets for articles you might be interested in writing—newsletters, trade magazines, and employee publications, to name a few.

BECOME A RELIABLE CONTACT
FOR REPORTERS

Send reporters who cover your area of interest your credentials for speaking on a certain subject. This may result in periodic opportunities to be quoted. Carla Marinucci, business reporter for the *San Francisco Examiner*, says that she welcomes such information. "When we have a breaking story or a new development in a certain field, I often don't know who to contact. I like to have the names of people I can turn to immediately for comments, for analysis, for quotes on certain topics in various fields. I think all reporters appreciate that kind of information and would welcome it."[7]

GETTING ON TALK SHOWS

Another way to get your message out is to be a guest on a radio or television talk show.

The Federal Communications Commission requires that all stations devote a certain number of hours each week to public service broadcasts. These may include talk shows, editorials, public service announcements, or informative reports.

Often public affairs talk shows are pushed into time slots when there are relatively few listeners. Asked if anyone really listens to the 6 a.m. Sunday interviews on his radio station, one public affairs director responded, "You'd be surprised at the feedback we receive. There are people out there listening."

Then there are many other talk shows on radio and TV that are designed as entertainment. These are programmed in more popular listening time slots.

Getting information about non-syndicated radio and television talk shows that are broadcast in your area requires some time and a lot of phone calls. Look in your newspaper for listings or look under "K" and "W" in the phone book for radio and television stations.

Telephone each station and ask for detailed information about the talk shows it broadcasts. You want to find out the names of the host and producer, the time of broadcast, and the types of topics used. Also request that brochures, program schedules, and other available materials about the station be mailed to you. Make a separate page for each station and put the pages in a notebook.

Developing a Media Kit

Your next step is to put together a media kit. Pick out two or three topics you have expertise in — your occupation, a special hobby, unusual travels. Use a separate sheet for each topic. First, list the topic as a title, then write a paragraph telling about your qualifications to speak on that subject. After that, list about a dozen questions the host could ask you.

Prepare a biographical profile emphasizing your professional accomplishments, education, unusual experiences, and other pertinent material. Include newspaper clippings and magazine articles that have featured you or that you have written. Your smiling picture presenting you as being outgoing and personable also should go in the media kit, which can be a quality folder with pockets. Attach your business card and display the material in an attractive manner.

Send it with a cover letter to the program director of each station you are interested in. In the letter, state your interest in appearing on the program (give the particular program's name) and briefly give your credentials. Be sure to include your phone number.

Wait a few days after mailing your media kit, then follow up with a phone call to the program director. If there seems to be a genuine interest in your topic and in you as guest and nothing happens, wait a few weeks and call again. A reminder may be all it takes to land you a guest spot.

Often guests cancel out at the last minute. If your schedule is flexible, and you would usually be available with little notice, be sure to state that in your letter.

Each time you appear on a radio or television talk show, be sure to send a thank-you letter to the host. Keep the door open for future appearances. Also, add the producer and host to your mailing list for news releases and article reprints. Use the Talk Show Information form below as the starting point for making contacts.

KEEP TABS ON YOUR COVERAGE

Keep a notebook of the news releases and contacts you make and include clippings and records of such things as public service announcements and appearances on talk shows. Also, track the results of your efforts, such as attendance at meetings and comments you have heard about each story. This will help you determine the effectiveness of a particular approach and will serve as an impressive record of your communications efforts.

Becoming thoroughly familiar with the media in your area and developing an eye and ear for material that will appeal to them can result in many positive stories and good publicity for you and your organization.

And that's good news for any group.

NEWS MEDIUM INFORMATION

News medium _____

Mailing address _____

_____

Phone number _____

Owner or affiliate _____

Coverage area _____

Assignments editor _____

Reporter _____

Columnists or specialized reporters

_____

_____

_____

Deadline _____

Public service programs

_____

_____

_____

Special features (community bulletin board, events calendar,

etc.) _____

_____

_____

_____

_____

4713 E. Main Street
Centerville, Colorado

NEWS RELEASE

Contact: Heidi Windham
(717) 555-8076

FOR IMMEDIATE RELEASE: June 30, 1993

CHAMBER TO SPONSOR PIONEER DAY

The Centerville Chamber of Commerce, in celebration of Independence Day, will sponsor a Pioneer Day on Sunday, July 4, from 1 to 7 p.m. on the Centerville Square and in adjacent City Park.

Featured will be demonstrations of skills early Americans used, many of which are considered arts and crafts today. Candle making, woodworking, weaving, butter churning, and quilting are some of the crafts visitors will have the opportunity to "try their hand at."

The Centerville Community Band will give a concert at 3 p.m., followed by a demonstration by Indian dancers at 4 p.m. and a performance by a Mariachi group at 5 p.m.

An exhibit of nationally known artist Candace Thomason's early American paintings will be on display in the Community Center.

The public is invited to bring a supper for an old-fashioned picnic on the grounds at 6 p.m. Cold drinks will be furnished by the Chamber.

Ending the celebration will be a fireworks display at sundown.

###

1356 Woodlawn
Shadyside, Illinois

PUBLIC SERVICE ANNOUNCEMENT

Contact: Earl Hampton
(815) 555-2479

FOR USE: May 15 – May 22, 1993

ANNOUNCER: (10 seconds) Introduce your youngsters to the delightful "World of Winnie the Pooh," to be presented by the Shadyside Players at 8 p.m. Friday, May 22, in the high school auditorium. It's rated "G" for great entertainment.

ANNOUNCER: (15 seconds) A real live treat is in store for your children at 8 p.m. Friday, May 22, when the Shadyside Players present the whimsical play, "World of Winnie the Pooh," in the high school auditorium. Call 555-2479 for reservations. It's rated "G" for great entertainment.

ANNOUNCER: (30 seconds) Introduce your youngsters to the delightful "World of Winnie the Pooh," to be presented by the Shadyside Players at 8 p.m. Friday, May 22, in the high school auditorium. Youngsters, young and old, are sure to enjoy this delightful classic, rated "G" for great entertainment. Refreshments will be served after the performance and children will have the opportunity to talk with Winnie the Pooh and his friends. Reservations may be made by calling 555-2479.

NEWS CONFERENCE PLANNING FORM

Event _____

Date of news conference _____

Time _____

Facility _____

Journalists to be invited _____

_____

_____

Date to mail invitations _____

❑ Notify UPI and AP day book editors

❑ Arrange for adequate telephones

❑ Check on electrical outlets

❑ Raised platform or sturdy tables for cameras

❑ Organization's logo on lectern or behind speaker

❑ Audiovisual aids _____

News kit:

    Background information

    Appropriate photograph

    Pertinent drawings, diagrams

    Copy of formal statement

    Copy of audio or video demonstration tape

    Host _____

Refreshments _____

_____

TALK SHOW INFORMATION

Station _____

Address _____

Phone number _____

Affiliate _____

Targeted audience _____

Name of program _____

Time slot _____

Producer _____

Host _____

Types of topics _____

_____

_____

Length of usual guest segment _____

Call-in format? _____

Date(s) of contact _____

_____

_____

7

Care and Feeding of Reporters

Media relations is really human relations. The more human the better![1]

FRANK M. HARLACHER JR., Director of Information, National School Boards Association

When a guest comes into a home, it is the host's responsibility to make him or her feel welcome. That's easy when the guest is Cousin Ralph, with his clever quips and "let me pay my way" attitude. But even when it's Aunt Sally, with her acid remarks and snoopy manner, there is a conscious effort to treat her as the guest she is.

ATTITUDE TOWARD MEDIA

The point is, there may be times when you are prone to dislike a reporter ... the way his newspaper handled the last article ... the one-sided approach that was taken ... the photographer's cavalier attitude ... or the lack of understanding on the editor's part. Whatever the reason, you should deal with reporters' visits just as you would with Cousin Ralph and Aunt Sally. Such visits are welcomed. Sometimes this is easy. Sometimes it's tough. But it is worth the effort.

Much of this chapter really deals with *attitude*. The proper attitude toward and knowledge about the media is essential for anyone playing the role of spokesperson.

MASS MEDIA MEANS POWER

Whether yours is the largest company in the area, or the most influential religious group, or the most generous of civic organizations, there is no way that you can have the last word in an article or a news story. The media may smell. It may be owned by a low-class dirtball. It may be the laughing stock of your town. But it has the power to say whatever it wishes about you and your groups.

Anything? That's right. Anything.

THE COURTS AND ADVERTISERS GUARD AGAINST MEDIA MADNESS

There are two shields that prevent blatant, outlandish media tyrannies—the courts and the advertiser.

Challenging the media in the courts is a matter of libel versus freedom of speech. Libel occurs when a report in the mass media—broadcast or print—unjustly exposes an individual to hatred, holds that individual up to ridicule, or damages that individual's reputation or earning power.

And no advertiser would risk being associated with a newspaper or newscast that consistently created fictitious stories. That is the reason you will not find major companies advertising in the scandal sheets available near the checkout in your favorite food store. These rags have to depend on sales resulting from their lurid headlines. However, the mainstream media depend on advertising and the number of customers of their news product they can attract for their profit and very existence. A healthy news organization must distribute information based on truth.

MEDIA MONOPOLY

Attitude must be a consideration, also, on the point of media monopoly. Unfortunately, most cities today are served by a single metropolitan daily newspaper and, perhaps, a single radio station with an all-news format. And while network-affiliated television stations present newscasts several times a day, few have the staff to develop many local stories. Instead, they follow newspaper and wire service leads. And in the smaller or suburban towns, usually a single small weekly serves the community, balancing a little news coverage with advertising.

So, wherever there is a news source, there is often only one in each category—radio, television, and newspaper—in a community, making news distributors basic monopolies.

If you don't like the meat one grocery store offers, you can go to another. If you disagree with the price of gasoline at service station A, you simply begin using the pumps at station B. But if you disagree with the editorial content of your local newspaper, there is rarely another choice. You simply have to live with it.

Sometimes newspapers and other news-gathering organizations like to think of themselves as hybrid operations, functioning as a private business and a public entity at the same time. While all are, indeed, in business to turn a profit, they can only do so if they keep the public informed and fight for the public's right to know.

With these things in mind—the media's power, safeguards against that power, and the monopoly-like niche the mass media has claimed—you can readily see that the best defense is a strong offense. Fix your attitude toward understanding that there is no way to control the media; all maneuvering must be done through *influence*.

BUILD A POSITIVE IMPRESSION

When you know a reporter is coming, make plans for the visit. While in reality, you know this is just an individual who knows little about your company or organization, it is also reality that the reporter represents the entire community, and how your business is described by this reporter creates perceptions.

Let your staff—from the parking lot attendant to the secretary —know that you consider the reporter a VIP. Greet the media representatives yourself on arrival, if possible, and make them feel at home. You should prepare a quiet, confidential area where interviews can take place, and check in advance on photographic requirements.

Tours often get tiresome for the host trying to impress the reporter and for the reporter who just wants the overview. Go over sites and activities with a map first, then let the reporter tell you which areas he or she would like to visit. Do not let the reporter browse alone. Provide guides if the event is an open house.

If the reporter has been invited to a function requiring tickets, be sure complimentary tickets are sent with the invitation. Newspeople are always guests when they are invited somewhere as part of the job. If several media guests are expected, prepare a "reserved" table or section just for them.

Introduce reporters to principals. For staged events, be sure reporters and photographers are seated "front and center." See that reporters have access to a telephone for a broadcast report, laptop computer data transmission, or facsimile use.

Develop a news packet containing:

- an information sheet about your company or organization (see below)
- name and title of person in charge
- program or agenda
- background or history
- people who have played significant roles
- interesting anecdotes
- importance to community
- list of contact persons and their phone numbers
- copy of prepared text of speech or statement

The prepared information packet will save the reporter time and effort in checking things such as names, titles, and addresses.

NEWS STORIES CREATE IMPRESSIONS

In dealing with news reporters, one quickly finds that encounters rarely result in a win or a loss. Instead, there are degrees of positive and negative perceptions produced by the story. Reader A may be influenced greatly in one direction; reader B, not at all. Nevertheless, reader A may carry that impression of your company, whether negative or positive, for years. Make sure it is positive.

Getting the upper hand in journalism has more to do with matching wits than it does with wins and losses.

ORGANIZATION INFORMATION

Name of organization _____

Address _____

_____

Phone number _____

President or head _____

News media contact _____

Number of members or employees _____

Purpose of organization _____

Brief history _____

_____

Major accomplishments _____

_____

Hours of operation or meetings _____

Affiliations _____

_____

Auxiliaries, special programs _____

_____

Chart, graph, or floor plan _____

Other locations _____

_____

8

Planning for Communications in an Emergency

There is no time during an emergency to read the disaster plan. [1]

NATE McCLURE

There may seem to be a contradiction in the title of this chapter. How can you plan when you don't know what is going to happen? How can it be an emergency if you have planned for it?

In truth, there can be no perfect plan. But through anticipation of problems — some can be foreseen, others cannot — a spokesperson can begin to learn how to phrase answers, how to take a negative and respond in the positive, how to set into motion a team of employees or group members focused on returning to normalcy, how to endear the most stubborn of reporters.

Robin Cohn, who was director of public relations for Air Florida during its 14th Street Bridge crash in Washington, says, "... your crisis plan is like an insurance policy—the better prepared you are, the less likely things are to happen."[2]

The effort of preparing for the media in an emergency does not come easily. It must be a priority of an office, a religious group, a civic organization, a hospital, a company, or an association. It must be considered with the same value and at the same time that an organization's backup plans are made.

WHEN YOU ARE THE SPOKESPERSON

Assume you are the spokesperson.

What would you be asked if your company were caught dumping toxic waste chemicals in a tributary of a river?

How could you react to reporters when they learn that the fire that gutted your church hours earlier was set by a close friend and a church elder?

If the hospital board on which you serve has just been alerted that a nurse was dismissed after three newborn babies succumbed while in the hospital nursery, could you face cameras and an interrogation by reporters?

There is always the response that, "We are still trying to get the details of the matter and once we have them, we will be happy to meet with you." Unfortunately, in an emergency, this "put-off" doesn't work. Members of the media are too competitive to decide that everyone is going to wait until they get a call from the spokesperson, then develop their story. They want information now, and they are going to get it now—perhaps not from the spokesperson, but from someone.

The reporter's cousin used to work for the company that is dumping chemicals. A quick call, and he can give the reporter the head of the trucking department or at least several truck drivers who, no doubt, have been involved in those dumping incidents.

Another church member knows a close friend of the arsonist elder and is happy to give the reporter that telephone number. Why, sure, he will just give her the elder's number, too. Who knows? The elder's son can probably give the reporter background information.

And if the hospital board spokesperson won't talk, the reporter will just get information from the medical examiner's office or an ambulance driver or a funeral home.

THE STORY WILL NOT BE PUT ON HOLD

The media may not get it straight from the "horse's mouth," but it will get something from somebody by deadline time. The point to remember here: it is far better to have accurate information from a top official in tomorrow's newspaper than to have rumors quoted there from an outside source.

Officials of H.J. Heinz food company found that out the hard way in 1985 when they refused to respond to allegations that its Star-Kist subsidiary had shipped a million cans of rotten tuna in

Canada. Their silent posture resulted in a 90 percent nose dive in tuna sales. President Richard L. Beattie said the company was "massacred in the press."[3]

When the emergency situation occurs, it is a waste of time to quarrel with a reporter by saying, "I can't imagine why you're interested in this; it's just a little matter between church members," or "Why don't you spend time explaining why tax dollars are wasted in the welfare programs instead of always reporting negative things about the school system?"

The truth is, you know little about what makes news for that media outlet in general terms, much less when it concerns a specific incident on a particular day. The media is well aware of what it wants to cover. It does not care about what you think on the subject. The reporter has been given an assignment. His only concern is to get the story by deadline time.

Hassling the reporter, refusing to return calls, claiming no knowledge, or minimizing the situation simply indicates there is something being hidden. Being too busy to return calls smells like smoke; denying something fans the flames.

Donald W. Blohowiak, author of *No Comment! An Executive's Essential Guide to the News Media*, advises: "Reveal bad news in total. The slow drip, drip, drip of damaging facts piques public interest and surrounds the story in an air of a drama unfolding ... revealing all there is to tell right off the bat allows the media to tell everything in one shot. The resulting bang may be deafening for a brief moment, but then it's in one ear, out the other, and quickly forgotten in the face of noise from other news events."[4]

High School Emergency

When the media is already hot, respond quickly with something cooling. As the district's superintendent, the top spokesperson, you respond. "We had a shooting incident at Julius High School this morning and two students have been hospitalized. Police arrested a teenager, who was not one of our students. We are now talking with other students who were inside the cafeteria and are trying to determine what happened. But the principal is gathering information and I will have a news conference this afternoon at one o'clock ...."

The reporter knows the incident did occur ... the situation is under control ... it is not being handled behind closed doors ... the superintendent knows the importance of immediate response ...

and more information is to come later .... It is not the complete story, but it is an immediate response from the top. And it opens more doors for the reporter to investigate before his deadline ...

- How many shootings have been reported at Julius High this year?
- Are weapons becoming a more serious problem than drugs?
- What do parents know about security at the school?
- What about metal detectors being used at larger high schools across the country? Are they working? Is this something to consider for Julius High?
- Has the arrested suspect been charged? How old is he? Is he considered an adult and can his name be used?
- What kind of gun was used? Where did he get it?
- Is he a dropout? Where did he attend school?

... and it gives you time to plan the news conference.

A News Conference Means Opportunity

By news conference time, although the police likely have handled most of the technical questions, you are ready to give the information as you have it. Begin with a statement about the shooting incident. Those remarks that have not been completely verified should be prefaced with "as we have been able to ascertain so far" or "at this point, we believe ..."

The conference is an opportunity to reverse some of the shock and anger. Explain steps the school has in place for a secure learning environment, and update student conditions (although the media will check to see if there is a change) with upbeat remarks, if possible. "Jeff's mom says he will probably miss the basketball games for a couple of weeks, but should be back in school on Monday."

Also, outline plans for working with the crisis team in dealing with student fears and frustrations.

The positive elements provided by the school should be included. Although they may be snipped from the videotape before news time, they may be elements that could provide a second day positive story, such as crisis teams consoling students or "a day in the life of a school security officer."

Use the conference to position the school district in its proper place. It is not the district that shot the two students, it was simply the location where the incident occurred.

In the same vein, in 1963, although much was made of Dallas's conservative image, it was not Dallas that shot President Kennedy. Dallas was simply a location.

PRE-PLANNING POINTERS

Pause for just a moment and think of a worst-case incident that could befall your business or group. Use the above fictional school shooting incident as a vehicle for presenting a proper way of dealing with the media in your emergency situation. Regardless of the location or situation, the business, organization, or religious group, a similar scenario could be planned.

Remember:

- Respond quickly.
- Don't deny what happened or be evasive.
- Have the highest official possible respond.
- Explain openly that information is being gathered and will be available at a specific time.
- Use media time to present your side of the story, positive facts that cast a more favorable light on your group.
- Prompt positive follow-up stories. If the emergency is a major incident for your town, the media will not let it be over in one day's news cycle. It will produce numerous features and side stories for readers, listeners, and viewers.

LUBY'S RESPONSE TO KILLEEN MASS MURDER

In October 1991, a man drove his pickup truck into a glass window of Luby's Cafeteria in Killeen, Texas, pulled out an arsenal of guns, and fired randomly at the noontime crowd. This massacre of twenty-two innocent people was the worst mass murder by gunfire in the nation's history.

The year had already been hard on the military town's 60,000 residents, who were distressed over losing more than half of their service personnel through Defense Department closures. In addition, several members of the community had been victims of the short-lived Middle East conflict.

Public relations professionals, however, agree that the manner in which the regional cafeteria chain handled itself following this terrorist massacre is a textbook case.

The response was quick. Almost immediately, the San Antonio-based company sent its chief executive officer to Killeen. He held a news conference the next morning. Not only did he thank the community for its support, he also announced an assistance package for those affected by the massacre. It included a $100,000 contribution to a fund for victims and their families.

The Company's Position

The company could have blamed the incident on bad luck. It could have elected to blame the gunman. It could have remained silent. After all, it too was a victim.

Yet, to its credit, Luby's took the high road. It was proactive. It had many audiences to consider, including employees and the families of the victims. Months later, when it announced that it would rebuild and reopen the Killeen Luby's, it had garnered considerable public support. The city urged it to reopen to prevent the vacant building from being a reminder of the tragedy that had touched so many.[5]

Matt Swetonic, a senior vice president of New York's E. Bruce Harrison Co., a communications firm, said, "I think it's clear from things that go wrong in the world that normal, reasonable people don't blame the company (in such situations)." The issue was not blame, according to Swetonic. Regardless of the circumstances, the "first step out of the gate has to be a quick response. They have to get top management on the scene."[6]

Another communications expert, Brian Cummings, president of Bloom/FCA Public Relations, said, "The company is a victim of circumstances, but you have to be prepared for the worst. The first thing to do is to get all the information together." He added that designating a single spokesperson as a media contact is the second step.[7]

ASHLAND AND EXXON—A STUDY IN CONTRASTS

Unlike Luby's Cafeteria, a chance victim of circumstances, Exxon Corp. and Ashland Oil were both guilty of negligence in polluting waterways with eleven million gallons of crude oil (in Exxon's case in 1989) and four million gallons of diesel fuel (in Ashland's case in 1988). The way each handled its particular crisis—and the resulting coverage and impact—were as different as daylight and dark.

More than a year after the incident, author Joani Nelson-Horchler said, "For Exxon, the tarnished reputation persists even today ... even after Exxon has spent $1.7 billion trying to clean it up."

After the Exxon oil spill, Exxon's chairman Lawrence G. Rawl was quoted as saying, "It's not really clear to me why everyone is so angry."

Contrast that remark with the candidness of John R. Hall, Ashland's chairman who thought it was only right to say he was sorry. He began several public talks with: "I'd like to apologize to all of you, as citizens of Pittsburgh, for the inconvenience we've caused you."

The company publicly acknowledged that it did not have written confirmation of all the permits before construction of the ruptured tank began, that normal welding practices were not followed, and that the tank was not subjected to a full hydrostatic test in accordance with current American Petroleum Institute standards. Ashland staff members also started briefing Congressional representatives twenty-four hours after the accident.

Apparently Ashland's proactive approach paid off. Only five days after the spill, the *Cincinnati Enquirer* ran a story with the headline: "Ashland Chief's Honesty Wins Praise." Ashland's stock fell off about $3.50 following the spill, but in less than four weeks, had gone back up to its year-opening level.[8]

Richard K. Long, manager of corporate communications for Dow Chemical Co., after a number of unfortunate bouts with the news media, acknowledged: "With enough bumps, bruises, and fat lips, one can decide that combat is not the best solution."[9]

A BAD SITUATION MADE WORSE

Officials of a suburban school district provided a classic example of how *not* to handle the news media when eleven-year-old developmentally disabled twins got on the wrong bus and ended up spending the night on the ground. In order to get home, the girls had to transfer to a second bus. That particular day, bus No. 5, which they had been trained to board, broke down. Another vehicle was substituted, but no one told them that No. 5 wasn't coming, even when they went inside and explained that they could not find their bus. Finally, not knowing what else to do, they got on another bus. At the end of the line, the driver told everyone to get off, so they did. They wandered around trying to find someone to help them. The houses, probably in a new housing development, were empty. Finally, they put their books on the ground, their arms around one another, and went to sleep on the icy-cold ground. The next morning, a man found them and called the police.

When the principal of the school where the bus transfer was made was questioned by a reporter about the incident, he replied, "I can assure you teachers were there supervising." When asked how the mixup occurred, he said, "I don't know. And what business is it of yours anyway? Are you a parent of any children in this school? If not, it's none of your business."[10]

PLANS MUST BE WRITTEN

Developing a plan for dealing with the media during an emergency is ineffective if it is not written and widely circulated among office personnel. And having a written plan is ineffective if it is not carried out periodically in drills.

While no one wants to consider having to cope with the detrimental effects of a catastrophe, if pre-consideration is not made, the community's perceptions toward you and your group may be negative and greatly magnified by media news stories.

In structuring a crisis plan, hypothesize the worst possible scenarios and circumstances. Then come up with the best possible outcomes to these scenarios. Work backwards from the outcome to identify the steps needed to reach that goal.

Set up a crisis committee composed of all levels of the staff to ensure that all essential input goes into the effort. Discuss thoroughly the pluses and minuses, the ups and downs, the safe areas and the stumbling blocks.

Talk through the plan, event by event, situation by situation, and develop a schematic that will help staff members visualize how the plan is to work.

Getting a Crisis Communications Plan on Paper

Among points to include in your crisis communications are:

Selection of a spokesperson. This individual must be a top official, highly visible, and capable of speaking at ease under the pressures of cameras, lights, heavy interrogation, and microphones. A single spokesperson means there is assurance that the organization is consistent in what it says.

Preparation and periodic updating of a fact sheet, background memo, or position paper on your organization. This will keep all employees pitching the same basic information regardless of the emergency requests. How many offices are there? How many employees? Locations? Phone numbers? Products or services? History of organization? Key departments and employees? Hours of operation? The list is limitless and dependent on an organization's need. Updating may be annual, but could be as often as monthly for some groups. Charts, graphs, maps, and floor plans may help describe the operation.

Assign specific duties to staff members or offices. The plan should make it clear who is responsible for what. Alternative people also should be named. What if someone is on vacation or out of town on a business trip?

Consider an on-site newsroom for the media. In the event of a continuing emergency at any site, often the media becomes "based" at the location for updating or waiting on further developments. Such a situation means telephones should be available for reporters. They may require a typewriter or computer, a facsimile machine, a copy machine, work tables or desks, and even an area for news conferences. Withholding assistance or making it difficult for the news people to work will be reflected in their reports. The more assistance the staff can give members of the media, the more understanding most will be of an organization's situation.

Designate an office or a staff member to keep detailed notes on the chain of events, recording the events and announcements whenever possible. While this initially may seem trivial and a waste of needed manpower, you will find it to your advantage to document the happenings and related comments and announcements. This not only serves as a backup to the media itself, but it also may provide insight for responses and reactions to future emergencies.

Make key people available to reporters. Although a single top-level spokesperson is essential, the media will want to talk to the individual closest to the action — the first to emerge from the jammed elevator ... the baker who first noticed flames at the rear of the oven ... the church minister who was traveling with the teenagers who disappeared from a youth camp. Such "witnesses" or "quotables" should be reminded before they face the media about what to expect. They will not be the authorities, normally, but will give the human element to a story—the "I thought we were going to starve" or "I prayed all night long" kind of reaction.

Work out a plan to keep reporters informed on the progress of a developing story. For example, in a search story, a "briefings" agenda could be set up for 10 a.m., 4 p.m., and 9 p.m., with information available immediately when something important breaks. Such a schedule allows reporters to work on stories they expect to file with their news outlets from interviews or photos taken in the search area. They then can plan to be on hand for the briefings as scheduled.

Identify all the critical groups with which you need to communicate. For example, a few years ago a church bus carrying teenagers home from camp was swept away by sudden flood waters in the Hill Country of Texas. There were family members, church members, schoolmates, and the immediate community to keep informed of the search in addition to the news media and the general public.

Decide who might be credible supporters and third-party sources for information and resources.

Plan how to assume a leadership position in seeking to solve a crisis and ways to communicate from a position of strength.

Keep media and contact lists up to date on a regular basis.

Update the plan frequently. People and situations change. A communications plan will do you little good unless it meets your current needs and organization.

Periodically review your organization's procedures and mode of operation to ferret out potential problems that could take on crisis proportions. Taking a proactive stance can save a group a lot of trouble and headaches in the long run. S.C. Johnson & Sons and Sears, Roebuck & Co. are cases in point. Floor wax and chemical maker Johnson removed environmentally risky fluorocarbons from its aerosol sprays three years before federal action forced others in the industry to do so. Sears anticipated government action on flammable nightwear for children. They garnered points with customers by voluntarily introducing non-flammable goods in their stores before the government ordered such action.

PRACTICE MAKES IT WORK

Once the plan for communicating in an emergency is developed, test it. Periodically try it out on a fictional crisis. Have staffers pose as reporters asking tough questions. When holes appear in the plan, consider them possible mistakes in a real situation. Build an element into the plan to counter these potential problem areas.

Luby's president Ralph "Pete" Erben said that when the disaster occurred in Killeen, he didn't look at the existing crisis management procedure. However, Ken Fairchild, a Dallas-based media consultant specializing in crisis management, says that too much went right for them not to have been instinctively following the tenets of an emergency plan. "It's only a crisis if you're unprepared," he points out. "A good crisis plan won't tell you what to do. A good crisis plan tells how to decide what to do. And that's exactly what they did."[11]

It is doubtful that there will ever be a perfect plan created for all possible emergencies and all possible media developments. But without a plan at all, you and your organization may be at risk of disaster and vulnerable to public opinion molded by an outsider—the news media.

EMERGENCY COMMUNICATIONS PLAN

Official spokesperson _____

Alternate spokesperson _____

Current fact sheet _____

Person in charge of on-site newsroom _____

Location of area for reporters _____

Documenter of events _____

Groups to be kept informed _____

_____

_____

Plan for making key people available _____

_____

_____

_____

Plan for keeping reporters informed on developing story _____

_____

_____

Updated media and key contact lists _____

Monitor for media coverage and public reaction _____

Plan for assuming leadership position in solving problem and for communicating from position of strength _____

_____

_____

Dates of emergency communications drill _____

9

News Media:
Prerogatives, Parameters, Perils

*Members of the press are free to write and publish what they please,
without fear of government censorship. This absolute immunity to
virtually all governmental oversight (with the exception of the courts
in the matter of libel) is a unique privilege, a tremendous responsibility, and an invitation to occasional abuse. It's a heady wine to
journalists, and it gives rise to smug feelings of omnipotent auton-
omy, insensitivity and delusions of grandeur.* [1]

DONALD W. BLOHOWIAK

The Supreme Court said the media deserves protection from libel
actions when writing about issues of the "highest public interest
and concern." The purpose of the First Amendment is to produce
"an informed public capable of conducting its own affairs," by pre-
serving "an uninhibited marketplace of ideas in which truth will ultimately prevail." In *U.S. v. New York Times*, a federal court ruled:
"A cantankerous press, an obstinate press, an ubiquitous press
must be suffered by those in authority in order to preserve the
even greater virtues of freedom of expression and the right of the
people to know."[2]

And Supreme Court Justice Potter Stewart said, "[The] pri-
mary purpose of the constitutional guarantee of a free press was ...
to create a fourth institution outside the Government as an additional check on the three official branches."[3]

Warren H. Phillips, publisher of *The Wall Street Journal*, presents this viewpoint: "All the talk about the First Amendment rights
of the press is not about special privileges for newspaper reporters

and publishers, but about rights of the public—the right to be kept informed, the right of the governed to have a surrogate watching the governors. The First Amendment wasn't drafted for the publishers' benefit but for the public's."[4]

Few Americans would disagree with the proposition that in a free society citizens not only have a right to know but must know what is happening. Most would also confirm that the news media plays the major role in keeping people informed.

However, problems arise in defining terms such as "truth," "freedom," and "fairness" and in placing limitations. For example, where does the public's right to know end and the citizen's right to privacy begin? Is it all right for a reporter to use illegal approaches in order to expose an illegal operation in business? Should protecting the innocent supersede the media's determination to give the public all the facts? Does freedom of the press include free rein to turn a court case into a televised entertainment program? Where should the line be drawn between the public's right to know and national security, especially in time of war?

While strict laws and codes of ethics govern most professions, the parameters for the journalist are not as clearly defined. There are many gray areas, and often, even if a court judges a reporter and the station or newspaper he or she represents guilty of libel, the damage has already been done to the reputation of a company, an organization, or an individual.

LAWS AND CODES

Of course, certain laws and codes do exist. For example, the Fairness Doctrine states: "Broadcasters are charged by the Federal Communications Commission with the affirmative duty to seek out and broadcast contrasting viewpoints on controversial issues of public importance." Under another heading, the doctrine reads, "When a broadcast attacks the integrity or character of a person or group, or an editorial supports or opposes a political candidate, the station must promptly notify the person attacked or opposed, furnish him with the content of the attack, and offer him air time to respond."[5]

The Zapple Doctrine requires a station to give candidates for public office equal opportunity to present their views. The exception is if a candidate appears on a bona fide interview program, such as "Meet the Press" or "Face the Nation." Candidates who believe they have been treated unfairly can file a complaint with the Fairness/Political Programming Branch of the Enforcement Division.[6]

Another consideration is the requirements of Public Law 93-380, which prohibits the release of certain information. For instance, unless parental consent is given, records or files regarding students fall into that category with certain exceptions: to other school officials, other schools, or an education agency, or in connection with a student's application for or receipt of financial aid. Law also prohibits the release of the name of a juvenile offender under legal age.[7]

On the other hand, records and most information from public institutions come under "public information," and the federal government requires that they be made available on request.[8] While this law does not apply to the private business sector, the news media in recent years have often insisted on getting information on the basis of its "right to know"—information that a business is not required to release.

REMEDIES FOR UNFAIR TREATMENT

Martha S. Reed, while a public information officer for the Port Arthur, Texas schools, said, "The First Amendment does not guarantee a fair and accurate press—merely a free press. Freedom of the press may be dangerous but it's the best guarantee we have to protect all other freedoms."[9]

But what if you feel you have been treated unfairly and inaccurately by the media? What can you do? What should you do?

In the case of a minor error, you might want to send the reporter a friendly letter pointing out the mistake and asking that the correction be filed for future reference.

If it is a major mistake or misrepresentation, then you probably would want to contact the editor by phone after you have notified the reporter. You can ask for a correction. This might be done in the case of a newspaper, although it would probably appear as a very small item in a remote corner of the paper. It would be rare indeed for a radio or TV station to make a correction. Even if it did, the correction would not reach the same audience that heard the original item. Follow the call to the editor with written correspondence giving the right information.

Another possibility is writing a letter to the editor explaining your position. Sometimes it might be even better to get someone who agrees with you, especially an influential person in the community, to write a letter to the editor.

If you fail to get any satisfaction, you might want to make a visit to the newsroom to talk with reporters and editors. If you go in peace, with the goal of educating rather than scolding, you may be able to accomplish your purpose.

You may be able to find a sympathetic columnist who will be willing to tell your side of the story in a column.

Write a letter or publish a newsletter that will represent your position and mail it to people who would be interested. A banker in a small Wisconsin town went one step further when a Sunday newspaper erroneously reported that his bank had lost money. After calling the paper, which agreed to run a correction the next day, he and several staff members visited area coffee shops to reassure depositors.[10]

As a last resort, in a really serious situation, you might opt for legal action.

TO SUE OR NOT TO SUE?

Jurors recommended in 1991 that Nellie Mitchell be awarded $1.5 million damages in a suit she filed against the *Sun* and said the supermarket tabloid had engaged in actual malice—reckless disregard of the truth—in publishing her picture with a fabricated story. The tabloid had run a picture of the ninety-six-year-old woman, identifying her as a pregnant Australian newspaper carrier. An editor of the *Sun* said he selected Mitchell's picture to accompany the article because he assumed she was dead. The tabloid's lawyers admitted that the article was made up, as are other *Sun* stories. Mitchell said that it made her mad, but that it was "so absurd I kind of laughed." She also got the last laugh.[11]

But not all libel suits have endings as happy as this one.

While you may be enraged by an inaccurate or biased news report, proving that it is libelous is a definite challenge. Libel laws vary from state to state. Basically, though, libel consists of two components—identification and harm to reputation. The burden of proof is on you that the story refers to you either by direct accusation

or by explicit implication. Harm or damage means that, because of the story, you are the object of public hatred, contempt, or disgrace, or that the false information had an adverse impact on your social or professional reputation and standing. Unfairness in a news story does not necessarily equate with libel, nor do minor errors.[12]

Public Figure vs. Private Citizen

The rules are different for a public figure and an average citizen. Public figures are not entitled to damages unless they can prove that the publication or station defamed them on purpose, showing reckless disregard for the truth. And the burden of proof is on the public figure rather than on the media. Citizens who do not qualify as public figures must prove at least negligence by the news media in order to collect any punitive damages.[13]

There are other considerations in making the decision to go to court. The medium you sue can legally inspect your records and affairs in order to defend itself. The time involved can become all-consuming. Of course, the cost of attorneys and continuing litigation can become burdensome. Also, even if a handsome amount is awarded, the case can remain in the appeal courts for years. And the decision may very well be reversed.[14]

For some, however, a matter of principle enters into the decision to sue for libel. Former U.S. Army Lt. Col. Anthony Herbert, who sued CBS after the network ran a story in 1973 regarding his army career in Vietnam, said, "I believe in a free press and its important role in our society. But I also firmly believe the press should be no different from anybody else—it should take responsibility for its actions, especially when they hurt someone. Why should the media escape accountability when everyone else has to be accountable for their actions?"[15]

THE INVESTIGATIVE APPROACH IN MEDIA

Author Donald W. Blohowiak says: "While expecting business to meet a standard of perfection, the press itself—with clear conscience—engages in practices fairly described as unethical, immoral, illegal or heroic, depending on one's perspective. Under the guise of press freedom and in valiant pursuit of truth, journalists sometimes accept confidential documents (that may have been stolen), pay informants, engage in deceptions, ignore summonses, refuse to identify sources of important information, report unsubstantiated allegations, betray confidences, trespass, and undertake other questionable behavior."[16]

In a 1991 exposure of three television evangelists, ABC's "Prime Time Live" used the following techniques: trespassed on private property while filming the interior of an evangelist's home, misrepresented their purpose and "problem" when attending a church service, said they worked for a ministry when they talked with the head of a marketing firm, and lied about their identity when they visited a home for children in Haiti. In the last case, when they returned to the children's home, they accused the proprietor of the home of lying about what he said on their previous visit and produced videotape to prove their allegations (which, by the way, also proved that *they* had lied).

The question is, should the media be expected to abide by the same ethical principles that they try to convict others of violating or should they have carte blanche to violate the law, the truth, and good taste with the rationale that the end justifies the means?

CBS correspondent Mike Wallace admits in his book, *Close Encounters*, which he wrote with Gary Paul Gates, that sometimes "60 Minutes" got caught up in the heady excitement of the pursuit and wound up with stories that conveyed more heat than light, more theater than substance. Painstaking research into the most minute details of an interviewee's background, klieg lights glaring in the guest's eyes, and Wallace's brusque interruptions, exaggerated facial expressions and gestures and use of his cigarette as a weapon were all carefully orchestrated techniques to unnerve the unsuspecting and leave him or her looking inept and guilty.[17]

Fighting Back

Wallace, however, was one-upped on more than one occasion. Dick Carlson, senior vice president of San Diego Federal, said he would participate on "60 Minutes" on one condition: if his own video crew was allowed to simultaneously tape the interview. Wallace agreed and was captured for posterity letting forth an ethnic expletive by Federal's cameras while the "60 Minutes" tape was being changed.[18]

Another interesting incident concerned a "60 Minutes" report on the Illinois Power Company. A sixteen-minute segment titled "Who Pays, You Do" investigated the power company's construction of a nuclear power station. The CBS show charged that "the nuclear industry in general and Illinois Power ... in particular, were plagued by uncontrollable cost overruns that would ultimately be passed on to consumers." Illinois Power, within a matter of days, produced a forty-four minute videotape called "60 Minutes: Our Reply." The power company had gotten permission to film and tape everything that CBS had filmed and taped. Their version incorporated the full network feature interspersed with film and narrative providing the company's pointed rebuttal. They also played the original film and tapes, showing how CBS had edited the final version to change the meaning of the original.[19]

A study conducted at the University of Georgia on the program's impact indicated that the power company's tactic did result in a decrease in perceived credibility of the original news source. However, the study did not show an increase in credibility for the representatives of the nuclear power industry nor for the Illinois Power Company.[20]

On the other hand, the Adolph Coors Company came out smelling like a breath of fresh Rocky Mountain air when Joe and Bill Coors decided to open their entire brewery to "60 Minutes." Union organizers had charged the company with physical searches of employees, confiscation of workers' personal property, misusing lie detector tests of potential employees, and racial prejudice in hiring. The resulting story, "Trouble Brewing," included glowing testimony from employees about their great company and was very pro-Coors.[21]

Mike Wallace said of the Coors piece, "... it was the critics of Coors rather than the brewery that came under heavy fire on '60 Minutes.' This was yet another example of a reporting team starting out with a certain premise and being led, by the facts encountered along the way, toward an altogether different conclusion." Joe Coors got a lot of mileage out of the story with a large advertisement in several leading newspapers across the country. The ad featured a dramatic headline: "The four most dreaded words in the English language: MIKE WALLACE IS HERE," then went on to tell the story about the "60 Minutes" report.[22]

A Tough Decision

Of course, the decision to face an interview with a tough journalist is not an easy one for a company to make. There is a definite possibility that the company may come out wounded and bleeding. However, a refusal may result in a reporter standing outside corporate headquarters saying: "We gave them a chance to tell their side of the story, but they were afraid to talk to us," and to follow that with whatever the company's critics have said.

Private companies do not have to release information to reporters. Donald W. Blohowiak says: "The 'public's right to know' is a moral force that drives some reporters to demand responsiveness from those they pursue. ... the press really invents this right when applying the concept outside government matters. A business should always reserve its right to determine its affairs. A company is under no legal obligation to speak to the press, although almost always it's in the organization's best interest to do so."[23]

Fred J. Evans, in his book *Managing the Media — Proactive Strategy for Better Business-Press Relations*, says, "While the decision to not talk to the press needs to be carefully considered, in general, this strategy is not as dangerous or futile as the press would like to have companies believe." He suggests three instances when it is probably better not to talk with the media.

- There may not be a story unless two views are presented. Without a company comment, the reporter may decide to drop the idea.
- A company with a monopoly on the information sought can certainly safely refuse to divulge it.
- A "no comment" response will be accepted by the media when there seems to be a compelling reason, such as the risk that innocent parties might be harmed or that lives might be endangered.[24]

While the news media tout the freedom of the press as license to investigate and castigate businesses, they seem to conveniently omit the fact that they are businesses themselves. Tony Schwartz, author of *Media: The Second God*, makes a provocative observation in this regard. "... we must remember that the networks are large multinational corporations. Without endangering press freedom, we must find an answer to this question: Should the networks be the major arbitrators and the most powerful spokesmen on economic, social, technological, and political problems?"[25]

THE NEWS MEDIA AND NATIONAL SECURITY

Marilyn A. Lashner, author of *The Chilling Effect in TV News*, said:

In the United States the Fourth Estate has historically served our democracy by functioning in an adversary relationship with the government. With a fervor born of self-interest romanticized by a sense of mission and patriotism, each party—both the press and the government—plays the role. Flexing its muscle, each acts to survey, stimulate, inspire, influence, or perhaps outwit or checkmate the other. And, as tradition would have it, the true winners to emerge from this vast effort are our democratic system and the public. It is the press-government adversary relationship that reinforces the promise of integrity in government and that promises to actualize the people's right to know.[26]

The question is, however, at what point does that adversarial relationship risk national security?

Secretary of State Dean Rusk told reporters during the Vietnam War, "There gets to be a point when the question is, 'Whose side are you on?'"[27]

And President John F. Kennedy was reported to be furious at stories about the planned invasion of Cuba. At one point he told Press Secretary Pierre Salinger, "I can't believe what I'm reading! Castro doesn't need agents over here. All he has to do is read our papers. It's all laid out for him." Later, after the Bay of Pigs fiasco, he chastised the news media with: "This nation's foes have openly boasted of acquiring through our newspapers information they would otherwise hire agents to acquire through theft, bribery, or espionage; … the strength, the location, and the nature of our forces and weapons, and our plans and strategy for their use, have all been pinpointed in the press and other news media to a degree sufficient to satisfy any foreign power."[28]

During 1991's Operation Desert Storm, for the first time, Americans not only read daily reports of a war, they actually saw the Middle East conflict being fought before their very eyes on the Cable News Network. But, as usual, another war was going on— the government's concern for protecting sensitive information and the news media's demand to know.

Paul McMasters, national Freedom of Information chairman for the Society of Professional Journalists, said, "The Pentagon went out with two fronts on this one—the battlefield in the gulf and the American media. I would say the Pentagon scored a decisive victory in both cases."[29]

The military had learned hard lessons in handling the news media from the Vietnam War when its credibility had been left in shreds. *Dallas Morning News* writer Delia M. Rios said of Operation Desert Storm: "Generals were on hand to lend authority and credibility to the proceedings. They were not defensive. They provided numbers of missions and allied casualties without straying into the enemy body counts that had proved unreliable during the Vietnam War. Above all, the briefers repeatedly invoked national security and the safety of allied troops to blunt probing questions."[30]

Col. Sam Floca at the Army War College in Carlisle, Pennsylvania, daily critiqued military briefings in his class for lieutenant colonels and colonels on "Military History and Public Affairs." He emphasized that "when the briefers spoke they were not only responding to journalists, their response was going instantaneously to everyone with a television and to the soldiers in the field."[31]

According to an exhibit on "The American Journalist—Paradox of the Press," shown at the Dallas Public Library, citizens were pleased with the approach taken during Operation Desert Storm. "The American people, judging from one public opinion poll, were quite satisfied with news as shaped by military briefers and thought military censorship a 'good thing.'"[32]

In the "Pentagon Papers" case during the Vietnam era, the U.S. government sought an injunction to stop *The New York Times* and *The Washington Post* from publishing classified documents concerning foreign policy that had been secretly copied by an aide working for the National Security Council at the Pentagon. While the Supreme Court conceded that publication of the documents might cause serious harm to the nation's foreign and domestic policy, a majority of judges felt that the press should be protected from prepublication restraints.[33]

In this case (*New York Times v. United States*, 403 U.S. 713, [1971]), the Court was explicit in describing this most vital of First Amendment functions:

> In the First Amendment the Founding Fathers gave the free press the protection it must have to fulfill its essential role in our democracy. The press was to serve the governed, not the governors. The Government's power to censor the press was abolished so that the press would remain forever free to censure the government. The press was protected so that it could bare the secrets of government and inform the people. Only a

free and unrestrained press can effectively expose deception in government.[34]

In a dissenting opinion, justices quoted President George Washington when he declined the request of the House of Representatives for the papers leading up to the negotiation of the Jay Treaty. "The nature of foreign negotiations requires caution, and their success must often depend on secrecy; and even when brought to a conclusion a full disclosure of all the measures, demands, or eventual concessions which may have been proposed or contemplated would be extremely impolitic; for this might have a pernicious influence on future negotiations, or produce immediate inconveniences, perhaps danger and mischief, in relation to other powers."[35]

And so it has been and continues to be a never-ending debate: national security versus freedom of the press.

JUSTICE OR JUICY STORIES?

The Senate hearings for Clarence Thomas's appointment to the Supreme Court and the rape trial of William Kennedy Smith kept viewers glued to their television sets during the autumn of 1991. But for some, it was confusing. Were they watching a sensational new soap opera or listening to a halftime commentary on who was going to win a sporting event?

In the Smith trial, the Cable News Network featured a bevy of legal analysts throughout the day to advise viewers of net gains and losses for each side in its play-by-play analysis of the court proceedings. ABC's "Good Morning America" featured legal scholars to pronounce scores from the previous day's action, and a panel of mock jurors hired by Fox TV's tabloid show, "A Current Affair," pronounced their judgment.

An editorial writer for *The Dallas Morning News* commented:

> The televised news coverage of the rape trial of William Kennedy Smith turned the judicial process into something more akin to a sports event and, in doing so, has put the television media on trial. ... It was the media circus generated during the trial of the kidnapper of the Lindbergh baby that got still photography booted out of the courtroom in the 1930s. It took decades before cameras were allowed back in many proceedings.

And only more recently has the video camera been permitted into the courts. Few can argue against the media's First Amendment right to be there. But with that right comes great responsibility, the most fundamental of which is to provide a public service. TV news coverage of the Smith trial failed in this regard.[36]

LIKE IT OR NOT, MEDIA AFFECT LIVES

During the 1992 presidential campaign, Vice President Dan Quayle, remarking on the failure of the family structure in America, chastised unmarried television character Murphy Brown for her decision to have a baby. His comments brought immediate reaction from women's groups, abortion activists (pro and con), child advocacy groups, and single parents.

The controversy aside, it appears even situation comedy characters—created by writers and portrayed by actors—have become role models and even heroes to a vast number of Americans.

As newspaper columnist Ann Melvin says: "The 'reality' of America — and of each personal life — is too often perceived through a square tube, darkly. The problem here is not men, women, babies, welfare or morality. Not even the presidential election. The problem is how all of the above is being shaped, willy-nilly, by television."[37]

This crossover from entertainment to news makes one wonder just how much the media creates, propagates, and decimates, rather than reflects, life.

Melissa Morrison, staff writer for *The Dallas Morning News*, writes: "More and more, according to some media watchers, journalistic fact and fiction are blending into a hybrid form of infotainment. And more and more, viewers and readers are having to ask themselves what's real and what's not."

Dr. Donald K. Fry, journalism ethics teacher at the Poynter Institute in St. Petersburg, Florida, found the disturbing thing about the Murphy Brown brouhaha was the fact that she was talked about as a real person. "In some ways, Murphy Brown is more real than a lot of newswomen," he points out. "She's crisper. When you write fiction, it's usually to make more sense than real life, because you can get rid of the shaggy edges."

Morrison attributes the increased mixing of fact and fiction to

"the result of a recent trend: younger people turning away from conventional media, such as newspapers and network news shows, to entertainment media for information on current events."

Media critic Jon Katz created a storm among journalists with his article in the March 5, 1992 issue of *Rolling Stone*. He contends that entertainment media grapple better with today's issues than conventional media do. He calls this phenomenon the "New News." He cited studies claiming that younger Americans are turning from "The CBS Evening News" and *The New York Times* to *Rolling Stone* and *Entertainment Weekly* for provocative treatment of social issues such as sexual harassment, the environment, and racism.[38]

Tony Schwartz says: "The media profoundly affect community attitudes, political structures and the psychological state of entire countries. Godlike, the media can change the course of a war, bring down a president or a king, elevate the lowly and humiliate the proud, by directing the attention of millions on the same event and in the same manner."[39]

The question is: Where does freedom end and inanity begin? The First Amendment in no way guarantees the news media the right to endanger national security, show little respect for the judicial process, break the law, and act downright offensive. Instead, it allows the leeway for the media to report what they believe news consumers want. Only then can legal means be used to cease injustices.

In the case of *Near v. Minnesota*, 283 U.S. 697 (1931), the Supreme Court wrote that no prior restraint "has become the hallmark of First Amendment theory." Of course, where journalistic abuses may exist, "subsequent punishment ... is the appropriate remedy, consistent with constitutional privilege."[40]

10

Face to Face with the Reporter

*Never talk to a strange man on the street if he is
holding a microphone.* [1]

ROBERT L. KIMMEL

No doubt any interviewee who has been thoroughly clobbered by a reporter would be green with envy at the way Chauncy Yellow Robe's interview ended years ago on WCAT, the experimental station of the South Dakota School of Mines.

In the interview, the Indian told of the warriors returning from the Battle of Little Big Horn. As he recounted the story, Yellow Robe became so overcome with emotion that he suddenly let out a war whoop. The intense sound level overloaded the transmitter and put the station off the air.[2]

Since few interviewees have the power to blow the station off the airwaves, here are some practical tips for doing the best job possible in an interview situation.

BEFORE THE INTERVIEW

Once you have agreed to an interview, there are several things you should do before the session begins to make the end result as successful as possible.

Learn About the Interviewer

Who is the reporter? What is the reporter's and the station's or newspaper's reputation for fairness? What is the audience? Is the reporter familiar with your organization? In the case of radio or television, try to catch the reporter's stories to home in on her style and stance of reporting. If the reporter is from a newspaper, look up and carefully read several articles to get familiar with his approach and method of obtaining information.

Be Accessible

First of all, try to be available for the reporter's phone call. If you are out at the time, contact him as soon as possible. Alert your staff to the fact that you consider the reporter a very important person and that he is to be treated accordingly. Recognize news deadlines by trying to accommodate the reporter in setting up a time for the interview.

Decide What You Want to Say

What is the overriding message you want to get across? Try to frame a statement in one sentence that will tell your story. You may even want to write it down and memorize it, so you will be sure you can speak smoothly and with confidence. Also, ask the reporter what topics you should be prepared to discuss. But do not ask for a list of specific questions you will be asked. The reporter wants your answers to be spontaneous, not sound rehearsed.

Don't assume that the reporter will ask the right questions so that you can present the information you desire. Having a clear, concise statement already prepared will help you weave it into the interview.

Anticipate Possible Questions

Cast yourself in the reporter's role and ask yourself what questions you would want answered about this particular story. Ask a colleague to help you brainstorm possibilities. Focus on the line of questioning that might come from a reporter who is not well informed or from an aggressive type who may ask abrasive and probing questions. Write the queries down. Then take each one and frame a concise, quotable response. Be prepared to field each question with a brief, well-thought-out reply.

Gather All Important Information

Be sure you have all available facts on the subject. Have statistics ready. Are there any charts or graphs available that will help make your point? Has anything been written that would provide the reporter with vital data? Think of good examples you might use to illustrate a certain point. Avoid being placed in the position of not knowing information that is pertinent and important.

Have an Information Sheet Available

If you don't have one, develop an information sheet about your organization. This should include, for example, a mission statement, number of employees (or members), number of people served or output of product, any kinds of special awards or recognition, other locations, and any other factual and favorable information. Keep it concise—one page in length.

Develop Rapport with the Reporter and Videographer

Try to get to know the reporter and the videographer (for a television story) before the interview. Be familiar with the newspaper or the station the reporter represents. Find out about other stories the reporter has done, particularly one on which you can commend him or her for a thorough and excellent job of reporting. Although the reporter is the one who contacted you and is in charge, the videographer also can influence the outcome of the television interview. Too often the videographer is ignored by the interviewee as though he or she is only part of the equipment. But remember that the videographer determines the camera angle to shoot and whether to use an extreme close-up. Probably, too, the reporter will discuss the story on the ride back to the studio with the videographer. Sometimes, if the reporter has to go cover another story, it is the videographer who will decide how the story should be edited.

Treat them cordially. Ask if they have time for a cup of coffee. Even if they don't, they will appreciate your hospitable approach. Learn their names and call them by name.

Decide Where You Would Like to Be Interviewed

Pick the spot that will be most advantageous to you. For a television interview, you may want to have your organization's logo in the background. Have in mind an alternative setting in case there is too much glare, noise, or other distractions in your first choice location.

Interview the Reporter First

Interview the reporter before he or she interviews you. Try to find out what story the assignments editor had in mind. What angle will the reporter be pursuing? Does it tie in as a local angle with a national news story? Is the station doing some type of series or a documentary? Why are they interested in talking with you? Will it be a complete story or a part of a larger story?

Help the Reporter Understand the Situation

Remember, your best protection against an erroneous, slanted story is a reporter who fully understands the situation. He or she may be new to your city or may not know any of the background. Assume that the reporter is rather ignorant on the subject. It is better to be too basic than to assume knowledge that isn't there. If you have a brochure or a briefly written summary of the subject of the interview, by all means give the reporter a copy. Keep in mind that silence is not a good option since it can appear that you have something to hide.

Use Setup Time to Good Advantage

Even if the reporter and videographer appear rushed, they have to take time to get ready for the interview. As the person being interviewed, you can use that time to good advantage by talking with the reporter. What you say during those few minutes can help plant ideas in his mind that will lead to questions that will allow you to say what you want to say.

Remember that When the Camera Starts Rolling, There Is No Escape

Be sure to ask any questions and give the reporter any information you think is important before the videotaping begins. Once it starts, it is too late to do anything but try to field each question as smoothly and effectively as possible.

DURING THE INTERVIEW—DO'S

Be Conversational in Tone

You do not want your replies to sound as though you are giving some kind of oration. Neither do you want your response to sound like it is coming out of a textbook. Think of it as an opportunity to go into the citizen's living room and explain your point of view or situation.

Maintain a High Energy Level

It is difficult to listen to someone who seems too laid back or very passive. The person suffers in the area of credibility and loses the attention of the listener. A reporter will pick up on an area you are excited about and may ask additional questions. An enthusiastic response may give you more time to tell your story, add details, and open up avenues the reporter had not thought of exploring.

Use Simple, Everyday Language

A news interview is not the place to display your excellent vocabulary. Newspapers are written on an eighth grade reading level for a reason—so that everyone can read them. A reporter will not use your reply if it is couched in language over the head of the average person. Rather, you will find your words rephrased in the final story in simpler terms by the reporter. It is especially important to avoid using technical terms, shortcut language within your field, and acronyms.

Mike Royko of the *Chicago Daily News* wrote an amusing column about his attempt to understand a Chicago school system bulletin. It was a simple announcement for teacher-nurse positions at the Walt Disney School. The description read: "These positions will provide teacher-nurses with an opportunity to participate in self-renewal activities culminating in a professional renascence which will determine for those teacher-nurses their personal desire to pursue their reborn skills within the Disney setting or to elect to carry on those newly acquired skills in a setting other than Disney."

After talking with an assistant principal and the principal, Royko still didn't know what it meant. He chronicled his frustration and confusion in his column, which ended with, "Who would ever have thought that a person would have to know a second language to treat a kid's skinned knee?"[3]

Use words and terms that communicate your message precisely and concisely to the average person.

Display Interest Through Facial Expressions

People will be much more interested in what you have to say if your words and facial expressions are a matching pair. A deadpan expression is boring and turns viewers off. Also, be aware that a shot of you with the voice of the reporter over the picture may be used when you are not even speaking.

Be Enthusiastic and Spontaneous

Even though your responses may be well prepared, they must appear to be spontaneous. Also, the way you say what you want to share may be as important or more important than what you say.

Acting experience may come in handy here. Even though you may be disturbed by the question, it is important to come across as being poised, confident, and enthusiastic.

Look at the Person Asking the Question

Never look directly into the camera in a news interview situation. It looks unnatural, awkward, and even shifty to the viewer, especially if the interviewee looks back and forth from the reporter to the camera lens.

Richard Nixon could have made good use of that advice before he participated in television debates with John F. Kennedy in their 1960 presidential race. While analysts who heard the debates on radio named Nixon the winner, those who viewed the program on television said it was Kennedy hands down. During the program, Nixon's eyes wandered around, giving him a shifty, insincere, unconfident appearance. Political analysts have named the public's reaction to the televised debates as one of the leading causes for Nixon's defeat.

A recent appeal on public television also illustrated the importance of keeping your eyes on the person with whom you are talking. The host was conversing with an "angel" who was offering matching funds for pledges made by viewers. The host, though, was looking at the camera while telling his studio guest how much he appreciated his benevolence. He came off looking strange and stilted, and it made the viewer feel as though he was thanking the wrong person.

Leave the Microphone Alone

The reporter will position the mike in front of you for your reply. Resist any temptation to reach out and take it or even touch it. The reporter is not about to let you hold it. At worst, it may come off looking like you are in a physical struggle for possession of the microphone.

It is the reporter's responsibility to make certain the audio is being recorded at the proper level. That, of course, involves knowing the type of mike and the distance it should be from the interviewee's mouth.

Remember that Honesty Is the Best Policy

It is far better to admit to an error or mistake than to try to cover it up. Reporters seem to take great delight in exposing lies and misrepresentations. The next couple of examples back up the wisdom of going the honesty route. Not only reporters, but also the public seem to respect the integrity of someone who admits "I was wrong."

When President John F. Kennedy acknowledged his responsibility for the Bay of Pigs fiasco, polls showed his popularity did not wane. In fact, it went up 10 percent.

Several years ago, Ford Motor Company recalled thousands of Montego automobiles because of faulty axles. They were not sure what the impact would be. Apparently, though, the buying public appreciated their diligence in not risking the safety of Ford automobile owners. After that, sales rose 77 percent.

If you made a mistake, present a plan for rectifying that error. Also, admitting a mistake removes the controversy, and the story may very well die a natural death at that point. Not admitting to an error will usually result in deeper probing and more media attention. That tactic also can get you on a reporter's "hit list," which is not a good place to be.

Get to the Point Concisely

Chances are, your interview for television news will last from three to five minutes. After the interview is edited, the story may last only about thirty seconds and your statement will be even shorter. You may end up with only one or two sentences from the entire interview. Or the reporter may talk over a sentence in your interview with only a part of the sentence of your actual words being used.

You do not have the luxury of being expansive and elaborative on a statement. Make your point with the fewest words possible.

Interrupt Rather than Submit to Unfair Questions

Don't be badgered into answering a question that you deem unfair, irrelevant, or inaccurate. Cut in with something like, "I would have to preface my answer with the real facts in this situation" and proceed to do so.

Aviator Charles A. Lindbergh used to respond to questions he thought were inane or did not wish to answer by posing this question, "Is that all you have to ask?"[4] Perhaps the average interviewee could not get by with that response as well as Colonel Lindbergh did, but it worked for him.

If the question is a blatant trap, you might even say something like, "I'm sorry but I really can't answer a loaded question like that." Then you can add "... but I will say ..." Whatever your response is, be sure you say it in a pleasant way.

Bridge from the Reporter's Question to What You Want to Talk About

Even though the reporter chooses and directs the questions, remember that you control the answers. You can briefly answer the question and, in the same sentence, expand the topic to include the message you want to put across. You can say something along the lines of:

"... but it's also important to remember ..."

"... and that reminds me of what we're doing in the area of ..."

"... while that is a problem, this is what we are doing to try to solve it."

"Of course, that's a challenge, but it's no greater than one we've successfully met ..."

Turn the Question

If the question is one you do not want to answer, don't answer it, but do so in a pleasant way that is not offensive. You can respond with something like:

"I don't really see that as the main issue here. The main issue is ..."

"I would have thought your question would be ..." Then proceed to answer it.

"I think most people are more interested in the ... and, of course, that's what we're concentrating on here."

Buy Time to Think of an Answer

If you are taken off guard by a question, stall for time to come up with a good answer. Ask the reporter to repeat the question. Or tell the reporter you want to be sure you understand the question. Rephrase it and ask him or her if that is the correct interpretation. During this exchange you will have a good chance to order your thoughts.

Remember Who the Real Audience Is

While you are talking with a reporter, remember that your real audience is not the reporter. The listener or viewer is the person your message is directed toward. Don't think about that one individual with the microphone, but rather about the public and what you want it to know. Your goal is to get beyond the "human filter" and reach the reporter's audience.

Avoid Answering Ranking Questions Too Specifically

When a reporter tries to pin you down to your number one priority or major concern, you would do well to hedge the question by making it more inclusive. You might counter with, "Well, of course, we have several very important priorities. Among these are ..." Then discuss one or two.

Charles Anderson fell into that trap when he first became city manager of Dallas. He was asked to name his top priority. He responded with, "Transportation." His answer created an instant personnel problem. Most city employees felt that his main focus should be on people, and at first they were very negative about accepting his leadership.[5]

Use the Reporter's Name in an Important Statement

Reporters are human, too. They like to have their name within the report as well as at the end. It makes them seem to be well-known and respected in their field. Addressing the reporter by name gives you a better chance of getting your priority statement included in the story.

Realize the Reporter May Have Information You Do Not Have

If the reporter brings up something you are not aware of or an accusation someone has made, be careful in your response. Be prepared to say something like, "I am not aware of a problem in that area," or "I will be glad to look into that."

Sometimes a reporter may have a predetermined mindset about the situation. In the case of an obviously erroneous belief on the part of the reporter, the person being interviewed must be very convincing to overcome the inability of the reporter to grasp the truth.

First, you might confront the reporter with an empathizing

phrase, such as, "That's very difficult to believe, isn't it?" or "That trend's been dead for several years." Or an even more forceful response, like, "Your story may already be written, but I don't believe it's complete" may help. Try to force a mental turnabout. Then back up your statement with solid facts, background, and reasons to drop the original hypothesis.

Be on the Offensive, Not the Defensive

Do not allow a reporter to put you on the defensive. Be bold, ensuring that you present proactive elements of the story. If the reporter surprises you with rumors, say something like, "I don't know about the rumors, but I do know ..."

Be Sure to Give a One Sentence Summary Statement In the Interview

Be aware that the anchor's introduction of the story and the reporter's comments probably will take up most of the time allotted to that particular report. There may be room for only one sentence from you as interviewee. Be sure it says, in a nutshell, what you want to leave with the listener.

Try to Get Closure on the Story

In a controversial situation, avoid giving the reporter the opportunity to keep the story going over several days or even longer. You do not want him to keep coming back and prolonging and enlarging on the story. A one-time negative story is not nearly as damaging as one that is reported on at several points and by an increasing number of stations and newspapers. Telling about a plausible plan to rectify a problem may dim the reporter's interest in a return visit.

Senator Charles S. Robb of Virginia unwittingly turned what might have been a one-time-only story on the NBC program "Exposé" into a prolonged dragging of his name through the mud in national newscasts. Three days before the scheduled broadcast of a story containing allegations that he had witnessed cocaine use at a party, told his associates to make threats to potential witnesses, and engaged in questionable personal conduct, Robb decided to go on the offensive in what politicians call a "preemptive strike." Through interviews and statements, he attempted to discredit the charges before they were aired.

Baltimore Evening Sun columnists Jack W. Germond and Jules

Witcover point out the fallacy of that maneuver. "As it turned out, that strategy was a world-class blunder. The denials served only to make a three- or four-day story out of one that would have collapsed of its own weight within a couple of news cycles. The evidence used on the air was too flimsy to sustain it any longer than that."[6]

Remain Calm

Take several deep breaths before the interview begins. This has a calming effect physically and gives necessary support to your vocal apparatus. Picture yourself as doing well. Be as well prepared as possible. Present a poised, unflappable facade, regardless of how you may feel inside.

DURING THE INTERVIEW—SOME DON'TS

Don't Give a "No Comment" Response

Avoid responding with "no comment" or "talk to my lawyer," especially if the camera is already rolling. That will almost certainly be used on the 10 o'clock news, particularly if you are scowling or shaking your fist at the reporter. Those types of replies put you in an adversarial role and make it appear that you have something to hide. It is better to be unavailable for comment if you do not wish to be interviewed.

Don't Question the Reporter's Motive

Questioning the motives of the media leads to their questioning your motives. A school district in the Virginia suburbs ended up looking very foolish because of its employees' suspicious reactions to a simple question. *Washington Post* columnist Bill Gold called the school after an amused parent told him that two teachers there were named Ford and Rockefeller. He intended to write a cute little item in his column about the coincidence. But when he called the school to confirm it, the secretary responded, "I'm not in a position to give out information to newspapermen and you'll probably have to call downtown." When Gold pressed on, she asked, "Why would you want to know that?" When he told her, she responded, "I still don't see any reason for your needing to know that. You'll have to get your information downtown."

He then called the personnel department, where he was

grilled by several people on his motives before a spokesman finally admitted that a Robert Ford and a Sidney Rockefeller were teachers at the school. What started out to be an amusing anecdote turned into an embarrassing eighteen-inch column detailing the third degree he went through and ending with the question: what does the school have to hide if it would react so suspiciously to such a trivial question?[7]

Ken Muir, information director for the Montgomery County, Maryland schools, has a motto and two questions for releasing information. The motto is: "Information is an attitude, not a policy." The first question is: "Why should I *not* provide this information?" He says those who ask instead, "Why should I?" can always come up with a lot of lame excuses. The second question is: "If the questioner were to go to court to get this information, would he win?" If the answer is yes, he says you might as well give it gracefully and save yourself a lot of headaches.[8]

Don't Clam Up

Remember that silence can be damning. In a controversy, a reporter's job is to present both sides of the story. In fact, the Fairness Doctrine states: "Broadcasters are charged by the Federal Communications Commission with the affirmative duty to seek out and broadcast contrasting viewpoints on controversial issues of public importance."[9] However, if only one side is available for comment, that is the one the public will hear. It is almost always better to present your case.

As Shelby Counce said when he was superintendent of the Huntsville, Alabama public schools: "I learned a long time ago that the best way to attract attention—from the press or anybody else—is to not discuss something that you don't want discussed. Because if you don't discuss it, somebody else will. Then you wind up looking as though you have something to hide. There's no better way to stub your toe than to try and tiptoe around something that you've swept under the carpet."[10]

Don't Ever Become Hostile

Unfortunately, there are television reporters who try to goad an interviewee into losing his temper, making an angry response, or becoming belligerent. Even though that reaction might be justified in light of the provocation, the viewer doubtless will never know that. The questions in all likelihood will be cut, leaving the interviewee looking like some type of maniac. The interviewee has everything to gain and nothing to lose by responding consistently with politeness and restraint. In the case of a live studio interview, the interviewer can come out looking like the bad guy when the interviewee refuses to take the bait.

A recent television interview with a representative of a school in Tarrant County, Texas is a good example. It seems that teachers had complained of their treatment by the administrators of the school. One of the administrators was shown on the 10 o'clock news shaking her finger at the camera and saying, "Now you turn that thing off ... right now. And I mean it. You'd better do what I say." It seemed as though the camera stayed forever on the woman, who appeared in the same league with the Wicked Witch of the West. No doubt the viewers concluded that the teachers certainly must be justified in their complaint.

Don't Make Any Remarks "Off the Record"

Assume that any statement you might make will be used. There may be a misunderstanding about what you designate as "off the record."

The Reverend Jesse Jackson found that out the hard way. In the 1984 presidential primaries, he told two black reporters that he wanted to "talk black" and went on to make an anti-Semitic remark. The reporters maintained that they had made no agreement, and, of course, the results for Jackson were disastrous.[11]

Even if there is a firm "off the record" agreement, your remark may tip the reporter to an unknown bit of information. The reporter probably can then find someone else to interview and get the same facts. Play it safe and do not say anything that might come back to haunt you.

Also, be aware that when a radio reporter calls for a telephone interview, the tape already may be rolling. Any flippant remark may end up on the air.

Don't Be Evasive

The importance of at least appearing to be open and aboveboard cannot be overemphasized. An experienced reporter will home in quickly on an area that appears to be upsetting or sensitive to the interviewee.

If you are unable to discuss a subject, explain why: "It's in litigation." "The accused is under age." "That's a secret of the trade."

Then say something like, "But I would like to say ..." and bridge to a point on your agenda.

If you try too hard to evade the area of questioning, the reporter, as mentioned earlier, may very well go to other sources and get the answers he is seeking.

Don't Give Just a "Yes" or "No" Answer

Provide additional information. Not only does it make for a more interesting interview, it also gives you an opportunity to elaborate on a point. Sometimes a reporter will ask a loaded question and try to get only a yes or no response.

Dr. Richard M. Adams, director of School Health Services for the Dallas Independent School District, shares his surefire method for guaranteeing that he has the opportunity to explain a one-word answer. "I always say, 'I would have to answer that with a qualified yes or a qualified no.' Invariably the reporter will ask, 'What do you mean by a qualified yes?' Then I get to tell more. It works every time."

Avoid Distracting Apparel and Mannerisms

Don't wear anything that might focus the viewer's attention on your dress rather than on your message. Avoid any sort of jewelry that might clank or move, such as a charm bracelet or dangling earrings. Also, shiny jewelry may cause a glare under bright lights. Men should empty their pockets of coins and keys they might be tempted to play with.

If you know about the interview in advance, you might want to wear a "power" color, such as black or navy blue, which speaks authority.

Avoid Saying "I Don't Know"

Even if you do not know the answer, it is better to respond with something other than "I don't know." Instead, say something like, "We're checking on that right now" or "I will have that information for you later today."

Don't Walk Away

It is better to stay and face the reporter in a positive manner. You may be able to override the impact of the story with your response. Or the reporter who is counting on a negative reaction may decide that there really is not an interesting story there after all.

MOST IMPORTANT TIPS FOR INTERVIEWS

- Plan ahead—learn about the interviewer.
- Know your subject—anticipate questions, gather information.
- Be open and honest, conversational in tone; use everyday language.
- Keep your cool—turn the question, buy time, stay on the offensive.

.

11

Being Interviewed on a Talk Show

... all those dealing with the media must present themselves in the most simple, uncomplicated, direct fashion possible. In the media all ideas, all images are weakened if they deviate from the necessary standard of profound simplicity. [1]

DR. JEFFREY LANT

Talk shows provide abundant opportunities to get your message across to thousands of people at one time. As a guest on such a show, you usually will have a better chance of getting your points across and knowing what to expect than if you are interviewed for the evening news. Many talk shows are live, and many others that are recorded for later broadcast are produced as though they are being broadcast at that very moment. That leaves out the editing process, and lessens the danger of your remarks being taken out of context or a sentence fragment being used, which might change the meaning significantly.

GETTING READY FOR THE INTERVIEW

Watch or listen to the show several times on which you will be appearing. Notice what kinds of questions the host asks. Is she straightforward in her questions or does she try to bait her guest and then pull out the trap? Is he chatty or is it obvious you had better have succinct answers ready? Does she ask for examples or seem to want just straight, factual answers? Does he give guests time to elaborate on a statement or move immediately to a new line of thought? Does she try to make herself appear clever at the guest's expense? Analyzing the way the host operates will help you to do a better job on the show.

Prepare a list of ten or twelve questions and send them to the interviewer before the program with a note: "These are the kinds of questions I am frequently asked." Also, include a biography and any recent articles about you or that you have written on your subject. Remember that talk show hosts are generalists and may not know much about your field. You also can use the time before the interview begins to bring out points the interviewer may want to ask questions about.

Decide in advance what you want to get out of the interview. What are the two or three main points you want to make and how are you going to phrase them? Have them on the tip of your tongue. Having your own agenda set in advance instead of just hoping the host will ask the right questions helps ensure that you will get your points across.

Brainstorm, preferably with someone in your field. What questions probably will be asked and how will you want to answer them? What questions might an uninformed person ask? What questions are you afraid the host might ask ... and how can you field them to your best advantage? Prepare yourself in advance for the worst possible scenario. Then you will feel confident that you can handle anything.

Find out the demographic information about that particular station's listeners so you will be able to gear your answers more specifically to their needs and interests.

Get someone to assume the role of the interviewer and ask you pertinent questions. This will help you to feel comfortable with the format and give you experience in fielding unexpected queries. Tape the staged interview and critique your efforts. Your goal is to sound conversational, enthusiastic, and spontaneous.

If you need statistics or direct quotations, type or print these on individual index cards to have ready for reference.

If you are an author, be sure to look over your book before the interview. This is especially important if it has been a while since you wrote the material. Can you imagine how embarrassing it would be to have a question posed about a section of your book and be completely stymied? It does happen. And it certainly tears to shreds the author's credibility as an expert on that particular subject.

Practice explanations in very simple terms. This is especially important if you are discussing a highly technical subject. Assume that your listeners know little or nothing about the topic. Remember that newspapers are written on an eighth grade reading level with purpose. A good measurement is to try to explain your program to a middle school student and see if he or she understands your message.

Arrive early for the interview. This gives you the opportunity to become familiar with your surroundings and perhaps the chance to discuss your interview in greater depth with the program's host.

DURING THE INTERVIEW

Time cues will be agreed on before the show begins. While time is the responsibility of the production staff and your host, you need to be sure not to get into a long, involved explanation when there is only a minute left in your segment of the show.

Kathy Kerchner, a television anchor and reporter for fifteen years, advises interviewees to boil all their great information down into interesting tidbits. "Interviewers want clear, concise, colorful answers. Don't try to tell everything you know. Instead, plan catchy phrases that will get the reporter's and audience's attention. ... any answer that goes longer than 30 seconds or a minute probably is too long."[2]

If you don't understand the question, don't hesitate to ask for clarification. If you do understand the question, but need a moment to come up with a good answer, say something like, "That's a good question" while you're thinking of a way to begin.

If an untrue statement is made, refute it diplomatically.

If you are asked a series of questions, pick the one you want to answer most and give that information first. Avoid simple yes and no answers to questions.

Don't get bogged down in a string of statistics or a long, drawn-out explanation. Get to the point. Use colorful language and examples to illustrate what you are talking about.

Be sure not to touch the microphone or its cord.

Kerchner observes that interviewers may ask tough questions and "play the 'devil's advocate.' They expect you to be able to hit back whatever they throw at you."[3]

Holly Miller and Dennis Hensley, who collaborate as fiction

writers under the name of Leslie Holden, did just that when a television talk show host tried to put them on the spot. He was asking them how they were able to develop a plot together, especially since they live in different states. They were explaining how they bounce ideas off one another and leave open-ended plot lines for the other to finish. Suddenly the host got a "gotcha" gleam in his eye and told them to develop a plot on the spot. They didn't miss a beat as they started making up a story about a television talk show host with a lurid past. As the plot grew spicier, he suddenly changed the subject—but not before the camera got a close-up of his sweaty brow accompanied by hearty laughs from the studio audience.

SPECIAL TIPS FOR TV

Of course, there are special considerations to keep in mind if you are being interviewed for a television talk show.

Always look at the person to whom you are talking. If the situation is a group or panel discussion and someone else is speaking, give that person your undivided attention.

If you specifically want to address the viewer, look at the camera. This approach would be used rarely unless, for example, the host gives you the opportunity to make a direct appeal for funds in a charity drive you are representing.

Keep your shoulders parallel to the floor and your head up straight.

While gestures are fine, be on guard against sudden, darting movements. Pity the poor director who has a tight close-up of your face when suddenly it disappears from view.

Unless you are accustomed to using a Teleprompter, do not attempt it.

Once the program begins, assume that your microphone is on at all times. When Ronald Reagan, a former broadcaster himself, was president, he relearned this important lesson the hard way. Thinking that his microphone was turned off during a radio address, he broadcast a tongue-in-cheek remark about signing legislation "to outlaw Russia forever," followed by, "We begin bombing in five minutes." No one laughed—especially not the embarrassed president.[4]

Be enthusiastic and use interesting facial expressions. Diane

Durham, who books interview guests for CNN-TV, says, "The expression on your face, the animation, the interest that you have in your subject is just as important in getting the information across to me as the knowledge of your subject and how articulate you are. ... They want to see something that grabs your attention, someone who is excited about what they're talking about. That excitement generates across the screen."[5]

Never look off the set, regardless of what happens, and don't look at the studio monitor. Don't ever assume you are off camera, even when others are speaking. The director is sure to go to a reaction shot of you just as you are yawning or scratching your head.

Watch those chairs. If you are seated in a swivel chair, resist the temptation to twist back and forth. Always remain seated until you are told you may leave the set.

Appearing on television can be an exhilarating and rewarding experience in more ways than one. Shirley Lawless, owner of the Book Mart in Dallas, says, "I can always tell when authors have been on a talk show. Customers call wanting to know if I have their books in stock."

PRESENTING YOUR BEST IMAGE ON TV

- Wear a slenderizing outfit. Television usually makes people look several pounds heavier than they are.
- Solid colors are safest for major clothing items.
- Shy away from white. Pastel colors are better for a man's shirt.
- Avoid fabrics of high sheen.
- Lightweight clothing will be much more comfortable under the bright lights.
- Shiny jewelry and anything that might make a noise, such as a charm bracelet, should be avoided. A necklace or tie clasp could cause problems by hitting a lapel microphone or the microphone cord.
- Men should wear socks that cover the calf and match their suits.
- Items such as wallets, glasses, and keys should be removed from pockets.
- Consider how your outfit will look when you are seated. For example, a short, tight skirt can be a disaster.

- If you wear glasses, you may want to spray them with an anti-glare spray.
- Don't button your jacket.
- Make clothing adjustments as needed before the session begins. Men usually will need to pull coats down in back because they hike up on the neck when seated.
- Don't overdo makeup. Have some powder handy in case you begin to perspire.
- Men should shave before an interview since television accentuates five o'clock shadow.
- If you color your hair, be sure your roots aren't showing. Dark hair roots appear even darker on TV.

12

Make News Consumption a Learning Experience

The independence and power of newspeople rest largely in their freedom to select news for publication and feature it as they choose. [1]

DORIS A. GRABER, *Media Power in Politics*

Learning how to handle the news media should begin at the point with which you are most familiar—when the media meets the news consumer. All of us spend time with the daily newspaper, listen to radio newscasts on our way to and from work, and generally watch a television newscast each night. Why?

It is not only because television puts pictures with what we have already heard on radio. Or that we need a new suit and look to the newspaper to see what is on sale. Neither is it because we just like the music, and it happens to be interrupted by a newscast.

WE DON'T KNOW WHAT WE DON'T KNOW

Most likely, we turn to the media because we know it knows something we don't—from a new store opening to a furniture sale, from a government coup to an approaching storm. And we know the media, by and large, are a dependable source of information.

As individuals, we cannot lay claim to information as quickly as the media can. After all, the news media are really a web of reporters spread across the globe, whose instinct and insight furnish an unstoppable supply of fascinating breakthroughs and simple yarns.

Nor can we even fathom the diversity of information that the media can produce. One listener may not care for the PBS (Public Broadcasting System) interview of a craftsman sanding homemade violins in Arkansas, but he knows something different will follow. Another listener is struck by the simple life of the craftsman and may literally daydream about it during the subsequent sportscast.

What's more, we as news consumers have neither the time nor the inclination to see and hear all that is available to us. For whatever reason, we seem to be "hooked on news," constantly entertaining and informing ourselves by reading, watching, and listening.

BECOMING A KNOWLEDGEABLE CONSUMER

You can use this relationship with the media to learn and to strengthen your position when, indeed, you become the active participant with the news media. Change your passive news consumer role into a media learning experience.

Absorbing the Newspaper

Analyze your daily newspaper. Where are sections and topics located? How much space is devoted to one story versus another? Watch for by-lines and begin keeping track of what reporters write. Determine which ones write business, government, sports, religion, arts, and features. Who are the columnists and who are the editorial writers?

By observing the writers and what they are writing, you will begin to be "acquainted" with the writer and get a feel for his or her approach. This is not only a valuable asset when you become the interviewee, it also puts you in a position of knowing the reporter when he or she does not know you.

Read the newspaper's editorials and get a feel for its bias. One of the more telling aspects of a newspaper's stance on various issues can be found in quotes. While short items may not contain quotes, most articles containing a dozen or more paragraphs will contain one or more quotes from the interviewee. Look for controversial issues and how quotes in these articles are handled.

A reporter may have talked for fifteen minutes with this witness or that newsmaker, yet elected to quote perhaps five sentences. He or she may have paraphrased much of the story, but what is selected as "coming from the horse's mouth" will—over a period of time—tell you something about the reporter's viewpoints and/or those of the newspaper itself.

And when quotes are used, what does the writer seem to like? Off-the-cuff quips or detailed explanations? Just the facts or emotional outbursts? Personal observations?

Did You Hear the Same Speech?

The next time you hear a speaker and know the media will be reporting on the speech, jot down your thoughts. Which quotes will the reporter use? What will be omitted from the story? Then compare the speech as you heard it to the speech as reported. You may find there are vast differences in the two. If there are differences in the speech report, consider how many more times in each edition there are stories reported differently than you would have reported them.

What about space allocations? Does a feature story about a company in another state get twenty column inches when a similar local story gets none? Why does this imbalance exist? Is it a newspaper problem or a problem of the company? Ask yourself if it is the newspaper's ...

- Lack of awareness of what is going on in the community
- Reliance on wire services for feature stories because it may be shorthanded
- Insensitivity to the local company and the workers
- Rebuffing because the company purchased no advertising during the last year

Check out other points. Do one high school's athletes get more ink than another's? Does one religious leader get quoted more often than another? Is partiality shown in reporting civic club affairs?

Does the newspaper often use an investigative approach—uncovering misuse of funds in local government, detailing an obvious unlawful bias in apartment renting, disclosing unsanitary conditions in a local restaurant?

Readers Individualize Newspapers

Finally, try this experiment with a friend or spouse. Open a daily newspaper and read through it. Have your friend do the same. Then go through the newspaper again and make a note of which articles you read and which ones the friend read.

You will probably find it interesting that while you read only through the eighth paragraph of the murder trial, your husband or wife read the entire article; while you skipped over the advice column, your friend skimmed through it; and while you read in detail the little note on computer software, your friend did not even see it.

That is the beauty of newspapers—they can be somewhat individualized to the reader. The headlines allow you to select the information you want or need and to skip the rest. News stories can go on for columns on some subjects without offending those who choose not to read them.

Start today. Make the effort now to get better acquainted with your newspaper. Knowing your newspaper, its political and editorial inclinations, and its staff can make you a more savvy interviewee. It can place you and your organization in a more positive posture when your story appears in print.

EXAMINING BROADCAST NEWS

The beauty of newspaper individualization is, of course, the curse of broadcast news. Only the newscast editor can select what will be heard by the masses. There is no individualization of news. Everyone has to hear the same thing and all of it.

Analyze local television and radio newscasts, too. Follow the same line of research, where possible, that you do with the newspaper, but there are some other things to consider.

Clocking the News

Occasionally use the time you spend watching the late news to your advantage. Learn more from the newscast than what the day's high temperature was. Take it apart minute by minute and note the items that were covered versus those reported in the day's newspaper. Take notes about what you can see and hear that takes place during a newscast. Expect to be somewhat surprised when you find out how much time is spent presenting each news item.

Using a stopwatch (or at least a clock or watch with a second hand), time a television newscast. Begin with the first news item and stop when the commercials begin; then continue when the news continues. Once you have calculated only the minutes and seconds spent on the news presentation, divide by the number of news stories presented.

Most likely, you will find that the average story is given about thirty seconds. You are getting what amounts to the first five paragraphs of a newspaper story before the newscaster goes on to the next item.

Basically, television and radio news are headline services when compared with longer, more in-depth newspaper articles. Few of us would sit still long enough for a newscaster to read for five minutes on a single story. So, while we may not get all the details, we do get more and varied stories in a brief period of time.

Did You Miss Something?

Next, check out the "sound bites" used from interviewees or speakers. Sometimes these are only parts of sentences, and their clarity relies on what the reporter says before and after they are used.

Businessman Carl Perry was pretty excited when he told a reporter how he was undercutting price increases: "Our suppliers have raised our costs by more than 25 percent. During the same time, however, we have cut personnel and closed earlier on Saturdays. And, because of these steps, we have held our prices to only a 10 percent increase."

But on the news that night he heard the newscaster say: "Costs continue to escalate throughout the area during this holiday shopping period, from fast food to computers. Carl Perry says his prices have gone up too ..."

(insert sound bite) "... We have held our prices to only a 10 percent increase."

Perry's efforts to lower the consumer costs were not mentioned, but viewers knew that things cost more now at his store. Perry may have thought the exposure would help his business somewhat, but after the newscast he held a different opinion.

As you watch the evening news, scrutinize the quotes used by the editors. Could there have been more? Could the interviewee have been cut off before his story was told? Was the story known before the interview was made?

Of course, most editing is well done, and oftentimes the reporter helps make sense of a selected comment.

Imagine You're In the Hot Seat

Now put yourself in the interviewee's place. If you work in a similar business or are involved in a similar situation, judge yourself on how well you could respond to the questions asked. Also, take a critical look at the person being interviewed and how he or she comes across on the screen.

Sometimes major figures, such as those appearing on network interview programs, are more savvy about the television audience perceptions. But during any interview situation—network or local —give a quick grade to the interviewee based on your own perceptions. Then analyze what makes him or her come across as a believable, positive person ... or as someone you would not want to sit beside on a bus.

Observe These Key Points

Watch for these points and determine how you could improve on what you are seeing.

Eye Contact. The interviewee should be looking at the person asking the questions. There should be no quandary about whether to look at the camera or the interviewer. The viewers are aware that two people are talking to each other, and they are simply watching and listening to that conversation.

Conciseness of Response. While a simple "yes" or "no" is rarely appropriate, interview responses should be simple and short. They should avoid phrases or words that are used only by a limited group. Every industry or business has its slang for internal use, but when the audience is broad, more common terms must be used for effective communication.

Poise. Too little attention is paid to this element. Yet more interviewees fail to be successful in their communications because they look uptight, they are nervous, they are fidgeting with their hands or twisting a ring, they are wiggling in their chairs—doing everything possible to call attention to their uneasiness.

Sincerity and Credibility Level. What makes an interviewee appear believable? Straightforward answers with no hedging. An eagerness to share information—even information that may be considered slightly negative—gives the impression that the interviewee is telling it like it is. And, finally, a little teasing or joking with the interviewer makes the entire situation less cumbersome.

Skill in Fielding Questions. Does the interviewee grasp the question's intent and respond appropriately, or does he seem at a loss to determine what the questioner wants? Whatever the question, however, a person who has practiced fielding questions can not only give an acceptable answer, but also add information to the response that is positive or that may bring up other areas for questions—areas the interviewee is more at ease in talking about or that allow latitude in responding.

Level of Preparation. The interviewee obviously knew he would be interviewed. Did he anticipate questions? Did he practice answers? Most people speaking on behalf of their organizations or businesses can expect some general questions, but they also should plan for tough ones. Ask yourself "how" and "why" questions about your group or company, and you will get a better idea of what a reporter might ask.

"Why has membership fallen?"

"How much time do you spend in research?"

"How is it possible that a child could slip away unnoticed?"

"How can your religious group brag about helping others when it gives only two percent of its collections for assistance services?"

"Why are prices up?"

"Why do you hesitate to cut services to non-paying customers?"

Fluency and Language Usage. Someone who butchers the king's English is considered uneducated. And an uneducated person is perceived as incapable of handling critical and unique situations. On the other hand, someone who is truly incapable of managing a situation but able to speak fluently, building strategies and points with the language, is often given the nod of acceptability. If there are small quirks in the language that continue to be barriers to smooth communication, such as double negatives and subject/verb agreement, effort spent in correcting the pattern will pay dividends time and again.

PRINT AND BROADCAST MEDIA DIFFER

So that there is no confusion when comparing newspapers and broadcast media, several points should be made.

Newspapers are in the business of distributing two things: (1) information and entertainment and (2) advertising. The former costs; the latter pays for the operation. Entertaining features, such as comics, cartoons, and columnists, are costly; news is even more expensive.

Broadcast media are in the business of distributing the same things. Some cost; others bring in revenue. But there is an immense difference in the percentage of money that is spent for broadcast entertainment and newspaper entertainment and that of money spent for broadcast news-gathering operations and newspaper news-gathering operations.

News is found throughout the pages of a newspaper, but news is presented during less than 20 percent of a major television station's day. And even newscasts are filled with commercials. What is more, smaller stations may have no news presentation at all.

LEARN FROM OTHERS' MISTAKES

There are classrooms available each day in the newspaper and through newscasts. Use them to check out the failure of others to communicate successfully. Make notes of how they could have handled the situation better, what their weak areas were, how you would have responded. Through constant critiquing, you will be better prepared the next time you are picked to be the spokesperson for your organization.

Postscript

Did you watch the evening news on television last night? Can you remember what the lead story was about? What other stories were featured?

What was the banner headline in this morning's newspaper, which you probably dutifully read before rushing off to other responsibilities? If you are like most people, you probably don't remember.

Even though the news media is a powerful force in our society, and we all want to come out like shining stars in any media contacts, let's take a final moment to put things in perspective.

Even if you do not come out to best advantage in a television or radio news interview or if the newspaper reporter quotes you in such a way as to cast a negative view of you or your organization and leaves out the extenuating circumstances, still it is not the end of the world.

Let's look at one major U.S. metropolitan area on a typical weekday evening when it is time for the evening news. A survey done by media people revealed the following information.

Of approximately three million people in the television viewing area, 1.5 million are potential viewers. The other half are out of town, asleep, working, or whatever.

About one-third of those, or 500,000, are in restaurants, attending meetings, in their cars, out on dates, and what have you.

That leaves about one million who are at home, awake, and potentially watching television. About 200,000 had the TV turned on, but they were not really watching it. They were washing clothes, eating, reading, doing homework, and participating in other activities.

That leaves about 800,000 watching television at that time.

with cable television, there are about thirty different choices in addition to videotapes.

About one-third of the 800,000 are watching the three major news stations: 125,000, station number 1; 100,000, station number 2; and 75,000, station number 3.

Only about four percent of the area's total population saw a specific story on last night's television news, and chances are, the next day, they will not remember what they saw. It is only there for a few seconds on the screen, and then it is gone.

Of course, newspaper stories are more lasting. They can be clipped, copied, and placed on microfilm in libraries. Even so, perhaps Edward Everett, a great 19th century American orator and statesman, can ease our apprehension.

It seems that he was approached by a man who complained that he had been libeled by a newspaper. The man asked Everett's advice about what to do.

His reply? "Do nothing! Half the people who bought the paper never saw the article. Half of those who saw it did not read it. Half those who read it did not understand it. Half those who understood it did not believe it. Half those who believed it are of no account anyway."[1]

Or as Vice President Dan Quayle commented about media attacks: "A fly may sting a stately horse and make him wink, but one is an insect and one is but a horse still."[2]

The bottom line is: do your best, strive to improve your news media handling techniques … and don't worry about the rest.

Pre-Test

Now that you have read the book, retake this true-false test. How did your answers compare with your first try at the test? The authors' answers, along with brief explanations, are found on page 142.

1. Legally you can ask a reporter to leave a rally you are conducting in a city park.
2. If you do not want to answer a question, it is best to say, "No comment."
3. Legally a reporter can be barred from a public school classroom if the administrator believes his or her presence would be disruptive to the learning process.
4. You should look at the reporter rather than the camera during a television interview.
5. A good way to postpone a negative story is to wait until the reporter's deadline is past before returning his or her phone call.
6. Every news story will usually contain at least one mistake.
7. To ensure that there are no errors, be sure to ask to see the story before the public does.
8. It is all right to give a reporter confidential information if you explain that you are speaking "off the record."
9. The average television news story is less than a minute in length.
10. The front page of a newspaper contains the most widely-read articles.
11. It is better to answer a reporter's question with a simple "yes" or "no" than to try to explain.
12. In a television interview, you should take the microphone to ensure that every word can be heard.

Answers to Pre-Test

1. FALSE. Since a park is public property, a reporter would not be required to leave any more than any other citizen would.
2. FALSE. It is usually better to take advantage of the opportunity to present your side of the story unless there are constraints, such as litigation.
3. TRUE. Even though a public school is public property, no citizen, including a reporter, has free rein to interfere with scheduled learning activities.
4. TRUE. A rare exception might be if you want to address the viewer directly. However, in a news interview, that segment probably would not be used.
5. FALSE. Unless you are the sole information source for the reporter, the story will, no doubt, be filed by deadline, and you will forfeit your opportunity to speak to the issue.
6. TRUE.
7. FALSE. An exception might be if the subject is highly technical. Then you might offer to look over the report for any error—if the reporter would like.
8. FALSE. Unless you want the reporter to get the information from another source or you want to "leak" the story, it is better to assume that anything you say might be used.
9. TRUE.
10. FALSE. Advice columns have the largest readership.
11. FALSE. Take advantage of the opportunity to get your message out to the public by elaborating on your answer.
12. FALSE. The reporter knows where to hold the microphone for best effect and will not let you have it.

Endnotes

Preface

1. Quoted by Jean Wiley Huyler, "Dealing Effectively with the News Media," Clinic, National School Boards Association Convention (1981).

Chapter 1

1. Walter Lippmann, *Public Opinion* (New York: Macmillan Publishing Co., 1950).
2. Source unknown.
3. Quoted in "What You've Always Wanted to Know About Working with News Media Representatives ... But Were Too Shy to Ask" (Dallas: Dallas Independent School District).
4. "TBS Cuts Back 'Good News' Show," *Multichannel News* (November 7, 1983).
5. Tony Schwartz, *Media: The Second God* (New York: Random House, 1981).
6. Ibid.

Chapter 2

1. Quoted by Mark Fishman in *Manufacturing the News* (Austin, TX: University of Texas Press, 1980).
2. Quoted by W. Lance Bennett, *News, the Politics of Illusion* (New York: Longman, Inc., 1988).

Chapter 3

1. Mark Fishman, *Manufacturing the News* (Austin, TX: University of Texas Press, 1980).
2. *Britannica Junior* (Chicago: Encyclopedia Britannica, Inc., 1961).

3. John Bartlett, *Bartlett's Familiar Quotations*, 14th ed. (Boston: Little, Brown and Co., 1968).
4. Quoted by Donald W. Blohowiak, *No Comment! An Executive's Essential Guide to the News Media* (New York: Praeger, 1987).
5. Quoted by Achal Mehra, *Free Flow of Information, A New Paradigm* (New York: Greenwood Press, 1986).
6. Ibid.
7. "This Newspaper Will Not Be Censored," *The Suburban Tribune*, Dallas (January 3, 1991).
8. Mark Fishman, op. cit.

Chapter 4
1. Irv Broughton, *The Art of Interviewing for Television, Radio and Film* (Blue Ridge Summit, PA: TAB Books, 1981).
2. "Anonymity of News Source Does Not Seem to Affect Story Credibility," *Social Science Monitor* (August 1984).
3. Erwin Knoll, "Don't Quote Me, But ...," *The Progressive* (September 1988).
4. "Role of the Source in News Communication," *Social Science Monitor* (August 1984).
5. Ibid.
6. Al Weston, *Newswatch* (New York: Simon & Schuster, 1982).
7. Ibid.

Chapter 5
1. Quoted by Jean Wiley Huyler, "Dealing Effectively with the News Media," Clinic, National School Boards Association Convention (1981).
2. Radio panel, Positive Parents of Dallas Seminar (October 26, 1991).
3. Craig Gifford, "Dealing Effectively with the News Media," Clinic, National School Boards Association Convention (April 1980).
4. "Listen to These Tips from Reporters," *The Executive Educator* (February 1979).
5. Ibid.
6. Quoted in "What You've Always Wanted to Know About Working with News Media Representatives ... But Were Too Shy to Ask" (Dallas: Dallas Independent School District).

Chapter 6

1. Jeffrey Lant, *The Unabashed Self-Promoter's Guide* (Jeffrey Lant Associates, 1983).
2. Kathie Magers, "Attracting Your Community Newspaper," Positive Parents of Dallas Seminar (October 26, 1991).
3. Ibid.
4. Dan Potter, radio panel, Positive Parents of Dallas Seminar (October 26, 1991).
5. Kathie Magers, op. cit.
6. "For Teachers, Pampering to the Maxx," The Dallas Morning *News* (November 27, 1991).
7. Interview on "Media and Bureau Relationships," hosted by Kare Anderson, National Speakers Association, 1991.

Chapter 7

1. Frank M. Harlacher Jr., "Working Effectively with Newspapers" (unpublished).

Chapter 8

1. Quoted by Donald W. Blohowiak in *No Comment! An Executive's Essential Guide to the News Media* (New York: Praeger, 1987).
2. "Crisis Media Relations Plan Seems Like Something You Can Put Off—But Don't, Says Ex-Air Florida DPR," *pr reporter* (December 10, 1984).
3. Donald W. Blohowiak, op. cit.
4. Ibid.
5. Pat Baldwin, "Massacre in Killeen—Communicating in a Crisis," *The Dallas Morning News* (October 18, 1991).
6. Ibid.
7. Ibid.
8. Joani Nelson-Horchler, "We Were Wrong," *Industry Week* (April 16, 1990).
9. Ibid.
10. Marilyn Schwartz, "Two Girls' Ordeal Changes Parents' Fear into Reality," *The Dallas Morning News* (February 24, 1978).
11. Steven H. Lee, "Crisis and Conscience," *The Dallas Morning News* (January 5, 1992).

Chapter 9

1. Donald W. Blohowiak, *No Comment! An Executive's Essential Guide to the News Media* (New York: Praeger, 1987).
2. Achal Mehra, *Free Flow of Information, A New Paradigm* (New York: Greenwood Press, 1986).
3. Ibid.
4. W.H. Phillips, "A Report to *The Wall Street Journal*'s Readers," *The Wall Street Journal* (January 4, 1982).
5. Irv Broughton, *The Art of Interviewing for Television, Radio and Film* (Blue Ridge Summit, PA: TAB Books, 1981).
6. *The Law of Political Broadcasting* and *Cablecasting, A Political Primer*, 1984 ed. (Washington: Federal Communications Commission).
7. *U.S. Code Congressional and Administrative News*, Volume 1, pp. 1-2040, 93rd Congress, Second Session, 1974 (St. Paul: West Publishing Co., 1975).
8. *United States Code Annotated Title 5, Government Organization and Employees S1-703* (St. Paul: West Publishing Co., 1977).
9. Martha S. Reed, "The First Amendment: Insure Freedom Through Responsibility," handout for mini-workshop, National School Public Relations Association.
10. Donald W. Blohowiak, op. cit.
11. "Tabloid Wronged 96-Year-Old, Jury Finds," *The Dallas Morning News* (December 5, 1991).
12. Donald W. Blohowiak, op. cit.
13. Ibid.
14. Ibid.
15. Ibid.
16. Ibid.
17. Mike Wallace and Gary Paul Gates, *Close Encounters, Mike Wallace's Own Story* (New York: William Morrow and Company, Inc., 1984).
18. Marion K. Pinsdorf, *Communicating When Your Company is Under Siege* (Lexington, MA: Lexington Books, 1987).
19. "Challenging Bias of Mass Media Can Decrease Credibility of Those Media," *Social Science Monitor* (February 1982).
20. Ibid.
21. Marion K. Pinsdorf, op. cit.
22. Mike Wallace and Gary Paul Gates, op. cit.

23. Donald W. Blohowiak, op. cit.
24. Fred J. Evans, *Managing the Media, Proactive Strategies for Better Business-Press Relations* (New York: Quorum Books, 1987).
25. Tony Schwartz, *Media: The Second God* (New York: Random House, 1981).
26. Marilyn A. Lashner, *The Chilling Effect in TV News* (New York: Praeger, 1984).
27. Doris A. Graber, editor, *Media Power in Politics* (Washington: C.G. Press, 1984).
28. Ibid.
29. Delia M. Rios, "Bad Press," *The Dallas Morning News* (March 17, 1991).
30. Ibid.
31. Ibid.
32. The Bettmann Archive, "The American Journalist—Paradox of the Press," exhibit at the Dallas Public Library.
33. Doris A. Graber, op. cit.
34. Quoted by Marilyn A. Lashner, op. cit.
35. Ibid.
36. "Smith Trial," editorial, *The Dallas Morning News* (December 12, 1991).
37. Ann Melvin, "Murphy Brown Fracas Touches Real Problems," *The Dallas Morning News* (May 23, 1992).
38. Melissa Morrison, "Mixed Media," *The Dallas Morning News* (May 30, 1992).
39. Tony Schwartz, op. cit.
40. Quoted by Marilyn A. Lashner, op. cit.

Chapter 10

1. Quoted by Donald W. Blohowiak in *No Comment! An Executive's Essential Guide to the News Media* (New York: Praeger, 1987).
2. Irv Broughton, *The Art of Interviewing for Television, Radio and Film* (Blue Ridge Summit, PA: TAB Books, 1981).
3. Mike Royko, *Chicago Daily News* (date unknown).
4. Irv Broughton, op. cit.
5. Ed Bark, "The Image Makers," *The Dallas Morning News* (April 6, 1989).
6. Jack W. Germond and Jules Witcover, "Unproven Allegations Aren't Fair," *The Dallas Morning News* (May 3, 1991).

7. "Why Would You Want to Know That?" *Trends for the Secondary School*, 1974.
8. Ibid.
9. Irv Broughton, op. cit.
10. Barbara Parker, "How Reporters Can Be Allies—Not Enemies," *The Executive Educator* (February 1979).
11. "Rules Governing Reporter-Source Relationship Are Becoming More Widely Accepted," *Social Science Monitor* (August 1984).

Chapter 11
1. Jeffrey Lant, *The Unabashed Self-Promoter's Guide* (Jeffrey Lant Associates, 1983).
2. Kathy Kerchner, "Preparing for a Media Interview," *Speakout* (November 1991).
3. Ibid.
4. Donald W. Blohowiak, *No Comment! An Executive's Essential Guide to the News Media* (New York: Praeger, 1987).
5. Interview on "Media and Bureau Relationships," hosted by Kare Anderson, National Speakers Association, 1991.

Chapter 12
1. Source unknown.
2. Doris A. Graber, editor, *Media Power in Politics* (Washington: C.G. Press, 1984).

Postscript
1. Source unknown.
2. "Lines for Our Times," *U.S. News & World Report* (January 13, 1992).

Resources

Bennett, W. Lance. *News, the Politics of Illusion.* New York: Longman, Inc., 1988.

Blohowiak, Donald W. *No Comment! An Executive's Essential Guide to the News Media.* New York: Praeger, 1987.

Broughton, Irv. *The Art of Interviewing for Television, Radio and Film.* Blue Ridge Summit, PA: TAB Books, 1981.

Evans, Fred J. *Managing the Media, Proactive Strategies for Better Business-Press Relations.* New York: Quorum Books, 1987.

Fishman, Mark. *Manufacturing the News.* Austin, TX: University of Texas Press, 1980.

Graber, Doris A., editor. *Media Power in Politics.* Washington: C.G. Press, 1984.

Lant, Jeffrey. *The Unabashed Self-Promoter's Guide.* Jeffrey Lant Associates, 1983.

Lashner, Marilyn A. *The Chilling Effect in TV News.* New York: Praeger, 1984.

Lippmann, Walter. *Public Opinion.* New York: Macmillan Publishing Co., 1950.

Mehra, Achal. *Free Flow of Information, A New Paradigm.* New York: Greenwood Press, 1986.

Pinsdorf, Marion K. *Communicating When Your Company is Under Siege.* Lexington, MA: Lexington Books, 1987.

Schwartz, Tony. *Media: The Second God.* New York: Random House, 1981.

Wallace, Mike, and Gary Paul Gates. *Close Encounters, Mike Wallace's Own Story.* New York: William Morrow and Company, Inc., 1984.

Weston, Al. *Newswatch.* New York: Simon & Schuster, 1982.

Blank Forms

NEWS MEDIUM INFORMATION

News medium _____

Mailing address _____

_____

Phone number _____

Owner or affiliate _____

Coverage area _____

Assignments editor _____

Reporter _____

Columnists or specialized reporters

_____

_____

_____

Deadline _____

Public service programs

_____

_____

_____

Special features (community bulletin board, events calendar,

etc.) _____

_____

_____

_____

_____

NEWS CONFERENCE PLANNING FORM

Event _____

Date of news conference _____

Time _____

Facility _____

Journalists to be invited _____

_____

_____

Date to mail invitations _____

☐ Notify UPI and AP day book editors

☐ Arrange for adequate telephones

☐ Check on electrical outlets

☐ Raised platform or sturdy tables for cameras

☐ Organization's logo on lectern or behind speaker

☐ Audiovisual aids _____

News kit:

    Background information

    Appropriate photograph

    Pertinent drawings, diagrams

    Copy of formal statement

    Copy of audio or video demonstration tape

    Host _____

Refreshments _____

_____

TALK SHOW INFORMATION

Station _____

Address _____

Phone number _____

Affiliate _____

Targeted audience _____

Name of program _____

Time slot _____

Producer _____

Host _____

Types of topics _____

_____

_____

Length of usual guest segment _____

Call-in format? _____

Date(s) of contact _____

_____

_____

ORGANIZATION INFORMATION

Name of organization _____

Address _____

_____

Phone number _____

President or head _____

News media contact _____

Number of members or employees _____

Purpose of organization _____

Brief history _____

_____

Major accomplishments _____

_____

Hours of operation or meetings _____

Affiliations _____

_____

Auxiliaries, special programs _____

_____

Chart, graph, or floor plan _____

Other locations _____

_____

EMERGENCY COMMUNICATIONS PLAN

Official spokesperson _____

Alternate spokesperson _____

Current fact sheet _____

Person in charge of on-site newsroom _____

Location of area for reporters _____

Documenter of events _____

Groups to be kept informed _____

_____

_____

Plan for making key people available _____

_____

_____

_____

Plan for keeping reporters informed on developing story _____

_____

_____

Updated media and key contact lists _____

Monitor for media coverage and public reaction _____

Plan for assuming leadership position in solving problem and
for communicating from position of strength _____

_____

_____

Dates of emergency communications drill _____

Index